York Excursions

0   10 km

0   10 miles

N

Stockton-on-Tees
Middlesbrough
Redcar and Cleveland
Staithes
Darlington
Middlesbrough
Guisborough
Whitby
Stokesley
Grosmont
Robin Hood's Bay
Catterick
Mount Grace Priory
Cleveland Hills
Goathland
Ravenscar
Northallerton
North York Moors
North Yorkshire Moors Railway
National Park
Scalby
Scarborough
Rievaulx Abbey
Thirsk
Helmsley
Pickering
Filey
North Yorkshire
Ripon
Fountains Abbey
Boroughbridge
Castle Howard
Malton
Yorkshire Wolds
Bridlington
Ripley
Knaresborough
Kirkham Priory
Great Driffield
Harrogate
York
York
Stamford Bridge
East Riding of Yorkshire
Hornsea
Wharfe
Wetherby
Pocklington
Market Weighton
Harewood House

8 9
10 11

York

Lord Mayor's Walk
City Walls
St John Street
Monkgate
Treasurer's House
Dutch House
Monk Bar
Jewbury
St William's College
Ice House
Roman Column
Minster School
Merchant Taylors' Hall
Holy Trinity
Bar Walls
St Cuthbert's
St Anthony's Hall (Quilt Museum and Gallery)
King's Square
Unitarian Chapel
Salem Chapel
DIG
Newgate Market
St Crux Church Hall
Herbert House
All Saints'
former Electric Cinema
Merchant Adventurers' Hall
Foss Navigation
Red Tower
Jorvik Viking Centre
Dorothy Wilson's Hospital
Wormald's Cut
Coppergate Shopping Centre
St Mary's, Castlegate
Fairfax House
St Denys
St Margaret's Church (National Centre for Early Music)
Percy's Lane
Regimental Museum
Clifford's Tower
EYE OF YORK
Bowes Morrell House
Crown Court
Walmgate Bar
Castle Museum
St George's
Dick Turpin's Grave
ST GEORGE'S GARDENS
Skeldergate Bridge
Fishergate Tower
Fishergate Paragon
Fishergate Bar
Browney Dyke
Rowntree Park

FOSS ISLANDS

Tang Hall Beck
Hazel Court
Alexandra C
Elvington Ter.
Lawrence Street

INSIGHT GUIDES

Great Breaks

YORK

Contents

Travel Tips

York's Top 10

From its awe-inspiring cathedral to picturesque medieval streets and a recreated Viking world – all embraced by ancient city walls – here at a glance are the top attractions of this charismatic northern city

▲ **York Minster** (p.14). This glorious medieval cathedral dominates the city. It's not only the most important church in Yorkshire – it's the largest Gothic church in Northern Europe.

▼ **The City Walls** (p.24). A walk around York's walls, the longest medieval city walls in the whole of England, provides some wonderful views of the city.

▲ **The Shambles** (p.42). Lined with drunken-looking half-timbered buildings, this is York's most characteristic – and photogenic – street.

▲ **Merchant Adventurers' Hall** (p.87). Dating back to the 14th century, this historic hall belongs to the most powerful of York's medieval guilds.

▼ York Castle Museum (p.48).
Step back in time at this great family
attraction, whose highlight is its
recreated Victorian street.

▲ Fairfax House (p.46). An elegant
Georgian townhouse boasting period
interiors filled with fine furniture, clocks
and decorative plasterwork.

▼ Jorvik Viking Centre (p.44).
'Time cars' at Jorvik take visitors on a
ride through Viking York, complete with
the sights – and smells – of the era.

▲ National Railway Museum (p.64).
Superb museum devoted to trains of
all types, including a replica of George
Stephenson's famous *Rocket*, the
forerunner of the steam locomotive.

▼ Stonegate (p.29). Picturesque
Stonegate is one of York's liveliest
streets, lined with shops and laced with
medieval alleyways that lead to pubs
and quaint teashops.

▲Yorkshire Museum and Gardens
(p.70). This refurbished museum tells
the story of York through objects like
the medieval Middleham Jewel.

An Eternal City

York, like Rome, wasn't built in a day, and this charming little city which bears the imprint of almost 2,000 years of history still manages to keep the fascination alive today

York is a city that encompasses all of England's history. Encircled by medieval walls and gateways that still bear the scars of battle, its great Gothic cathedral lies surrounded by quaint narrow streets. The bustling life of the golden Elizabethan age can be imagined in the half-timbered houses of the Shambles and the elegance of Georgian England savoured in the sleek lines and fine furniture of Fairfax House. The power and authority of ancient Rome can be glimpsed in the remains of legionary fortress walls, and the all-conquering Vikings have left the wooden walls of their Jorvik settlement in Coppergate. 'The history of York is the history of England,' declared George VI.

York has seen invaders come and go. Battles have raged around its sturdy walls and kings and queens have demanded entry at its gates. And the city has withstood them all, though each age has left some legacy of its passing. Happily though, the heart of

the city somehow managed to escape the attentions of the Industrial Revolution, with the railway station firmly sited just outside the walls. The result is a very modern 'medieval' city; one that is able to illustrate its own intriguing story through its streets, its buildings and its stained glass. It has become a compelling mixture of all former ages with some 21st-century additions. And despite all the temptations created by tourism, it remains a living city – a tourist honey pot yes, but one that resolutely refuses to turn itself into a museum.

LANDSCAPE AND LOCATION

The city straddles the River Ouse and dominates the Plain of York. It stands halfway between London and Edinburgh and has, since early times, been the home of the Archbishop of York, the Primate of England, who is second only to the Archbishop of Canterbury in the hierarchy of the Anglican Church. When Yorkshire was one

Above: along the River Ouse waterfront. **Below**: inside the Minster, York's Gothic masterpiece.

Above: remains of Roman York, which was known as Eboracum.

county, York was the county town – ideally placed where the three ridings or administrative areas converged. Since 1963 it has also been a university city with a growing reputation as a centre of academic excellence.

For the success of its geographical location the city can thank the Romans, who picked the spot with their usual practicality. The Ouse provided them with access to the sea and the confluence with the River Foss gave their fortress water protection on two sides. When the legions marched away, Anglo-Saxon and then Viking invaders saw the strategic convenience of the site and moved in. Centuries later, York was on the coaching route between London and Scotland, and later still George Hudson, the city's Railway King, made certain that the main line north passed his city.

ECONOMY

York's road and river links quickly established it as a trading centre. Even in Roman times, ships with wine from Bordeaux were docking at its quays. Medieval merchants set up a powerful Merchant Adventurers' trading company. Specialist markets dealing in butter, meat, animals and hay so crowded the streets that houses, even church graveyards, were demolished to give the traders more room. For miles around, York was the place to go to sell and buy.

But the city slowly lost out economically to the industrial towns of the West Riding. York came to rely on a mixture of railways and chocolate for its prosperity. Two famous confectionery firms, Rowntree and Terry's, were the main sources of employment, along with the building of railway coaches at the headquarters of the London and North Eastern Railway Company. For a time, York became a backwater and assumed a genteel shabbiness before making a post-war revival through tourism – an industry which now pours millions of pounds into the city.

Above: the clock at York's 19th-century railway station.

Such was the concern that historic cities could be destroyed by commercial pressures that in 1968 York was chosen for a special study by the town planner Viscount Esher. Not all his ideas were adopted, but gradually city-centre traffic was controlled, then excluded – a far-seeing move that makes the York of today a pedestrian-friendly, clean, green city, with a well-organised park-and-ride scheme.

Above: a busy day of shopping on the pedestrianised Shambles.

ARCHAEOLOGY

Ironically, it is York's past that has provided the basis for its present prosperity. Knock down any building in central York and you will find another underneath it – each presenting a perfect opportunity for finding out more about the city's history.

Over the years organisations and individuals have fought hard to preserve the city. In the early 19th century, the city fathers wanted to pull down the Bar Walls and sell off the stone, and there was pressure for the removal of ancient gateways, which were considered obstacles to trade. Protest groups saved the gateways but not all the barbicans: only one survives, at Walmgate.

York was fortunate not to be badly scarred by post-World War II reconstruction work. The York Civic Trust led a battle to protect the city's old buildings from demolition and proposed instead careful renovation and adaptation to new uses. Their plea was to preserve the city's uniqueness.

The York Archaeological Trust has proved the value of 'rescue archaeology', where archaeologists are given time to dig ahead of new building work. When Viking York was discovered under Coppergate, the Trust showed that archaeology, far from holding up development, could lead to profitable commercial ventures. The Jorvik Viking Centre, created by the Trust on the site of the dig, has paid for itself. Thanks to the Archaeological Trust a great deal of light has also been shed on the Dark Ages in York. Information has been gathered from seeds, pollen, fragments of bone, pieces of wood – even snail shells. The eating habits and lifestyle of Viking York have been revealed through the richness of its floor 'droppings'.

Hungate, an area to the east of the city centre, was the most recent area to be excavated and its findings are on show at DIG *(see p.81)*. Completed in 2011, it revealed fascinating artefacts that add even more to the story of the history of York.

Guide to Coloured Boxes

E Eating	This guide is dotted with coloured boxes providing additional practical and cultural information to make the most of your visit. Here is a guide to the coding system.
F Fact	
G Green	
K Kids	
S Shopping	
V View	

Food and Drink

There's no shortage of places to eat and drink in York. You can find everything from Turkish cuisine to tapas, Indian food to Italian – not forgetting, of course, traditional English dishes, which are most likely to be found in pubs.

As in other British cities, vegetarians are generally well catered for (despite the 'meatiness' of the traditional Yorkshire diet) and restaurants, pubs and cafés are all likely to have at least one vegetarian option on the menu.

Above: when in York, a visit to Bettys tea rooms is a must.

LOCAL SPECIALITY FOODS

In recent years there has been a welcome move for eating establishments in and around the city to feature locally sourced produce on their menus. Consequently, you might well find Yorkshire rare-bred beef, trout from nearby Pickering, tender pink rhubarb from the Rhubarb Triangle in West Yorkshire (which recently

Below: Yorkshire puddings are a local speciality.

gained European Protected Designation of Origin status, alongside fine foods like parmesan), as well as delicious Yorkshire cheeses.

York has two claims to culinary fame: York ham and Yorkshire puddings. What differentiates York ham is a type of curing that involves salt and light smoking. Folklore suggests the name came about because oak shavings from the building of the Minster were used for smoking.

Yorkshire puddings have become the traditional accompaniment to that iconic English meal of roast beef, roast potatoes and horseradish sauce. Most cafés and pubs in and around the city have them on their menus, usually served with onion gravy. A simple batter of flour, eggs and milk cooked in the oven, Yorkshire pudding is cheap to make and extremely filling, so it was originally eaten with gravy as a starter. This ensured that a hungry family had less appetite for the more expensive meat dish – allowing thrifty housewives to eke out their budget. It can also be eaten as a sweet course, topped with jam instead of gravy.

You will also find bakers selling Yorkshire parkin. This dark, spicy

ⓢ York's Chocolate Trail

Pick up a map in the tourist office in Museum Street and follow York's Chocolate Trail, which maps out all things chocolate. Think York, think chocolate; names like Rowntree's and Terry's, plus other Quaker families making confectionery, are deeply rooted in York's social and industrial development. Follow the history trail and also visit themed cafés and individual chocolate shops. The trail ends at York's Chocolate Story in King's Square *(see p.76)*. The York Chocolate Festival takes place in early April.

Above: assorted gourmet chocolates in different shapes and colours.

version of gingerbread is made with treacle and is frequently eaten on Bonfire Night – often with a crumbly piece of cheese.

An elegant lunch in York can be savoured at **Bettys** in St Helen's Square *(see p.39)*, but if all you want is a snack, you will be able to choose from a bewildering selection of city-centre pubs offering sandwiches, shepherd's pies and the usual chips-with-everything fare. Now there is also a host of upmarket coffee bars.

Some country cafés still serve Yorkshire high teas, substantial affairs involving fried ham, eggs and sausages followed by apple pie and cheese. Even ordinary teas are generous, often involving spiced tea cakes and 'fat rascals', large scone-like buns packed full of dried fruit and cherries. Always accompanied, of course, by a pot of strong Yorkshire tea.

ALE RULES

York is a great destination for anyone who loves real ale – that's traditional cask-conditioned ale. There are a number of breweries in Yorkshire, so look out for beers produced by

the city's York Brewery, Black Sheep Brewery and Theakston's Brewery in the Dales, Daleside Brewery in Harrogate, Hambleton Ales from Melmerby and Rooster's Brewery from Knaresborough. Pubs worth checking out include the Rook and Gaskill and the Waggon and Horses (both in Lawrence St) and the Phoenix (George Street). In mid-September, real ales are celebrated in an annual York Beer and Cider Festival (www. yorkbeerfestival.org.uk).

Driving out into York's countryside, you will find a host of attractive village pubs offering real ales and good, home-cooked food in a tranquil setting.

Find our recommended restaurants at the end of each Tour. Below is a Price Guide to help you make your choice.

Eating Out Price Guide

Two-course meal for one person, including a glass of wine.

£££	over £30
££	£15–30
£	under £15

Tour 1

The Heart of York

This walk focuses on the Gothic heart of York – the Minster. At under 2 miles (3.2km) long, it could be completed in half a day, but there's so much of interest you'll want a full day

This tour covers just a small corner of the city, but encompasses almost 2,000 years of history, giving you the opportunity to see everything from Roman remains to 20th-century artworks. Not bad for one day.

It starts at York's fabulous Gothic cathedral, the mother church for England's 'Northern Province', erected on a site once occupied by a Roman fort. It has many treasures, most notably its fine stained glass. The walk then takes you around the environs of the Minster, including St William's College and Treasurer's House, before climbing up onto the medieval walls at Monk Bar for a picturesque walk along the ramparts and a semi-aerial view of the Old City. The walk ends at the city's Art Gallery, whose paintings span 600 years.

Highlights

- The Minster
- St William's College
- Minster Library
- Treasurer's House
- Monk Bar
- Bootham Bar
- York Art Gallery

THE MINSTER

The Minster ❶ (tel: 01904 557 200; www.yorkminster.org; Mon–Sat 9am–5pm (last entry), Sun noon–5pm; services throughout the day from 7am; guided tours; charge) is the largest Gothic cathedral north of the Alps and is both a cathedral and a minster

Preceding Pages: the stunning dome inside the Minster's Chapter House. **Left and Above**: the Minster's Gothic towers and east door.

A long-spanning history

The history of the Minster is the history of England. A Roman legion's headquarters stood here from AD71 before the first wooden church was founded in 627; it was named for St Peter (as the cathedral still is today) and was built for the baptism of the Anglo-Saxon King Edwin of Northumbria. It was almost immediately rebuilt in stone, but this was damaged by fire in 1069, when the Normans came to York. Between 1080 and 1100, work was carried out on a new Minster, which was much altered and enlarged over the years. In 1295 work began on the Nave – and continued for 70 years. The word 'nave' comes from the Latin for ship, *navis* and likens the cathedral to a vessel of salvation. The present Gothic cathedral was finally completed in 1472, and took more than 250 years to build.

There was major restoration after two serious 19th-century fires. In 1829 a religious fanatic, Jonathan Martin, set fire to the choir (quire) area, destroying its stalls and roof. A workman's candle set fire to the South West Tower in 1840 and severely damaged the nave. A third fire – thought to have been caused by lightning in 1984 – destroyed the South Transept roof. It occurred just three days after controversial clergyman David Jenkins had been consecrated Bishop

– a cathedral because of its Archbishop's Throne and a minster because it has been served since Saxon times by a team of clergy. It has the widest nave in England, stands 197ft (60m) high, is 518ft (158m) long and 249ft (76m) wide across the transepts. Despite its size, recent restorations and cleaning give the visitor an impression of airy lightness. Its dimensions may make an immediate impression, but its ornate detail makes it an attraction worth spending an entire day exploring.

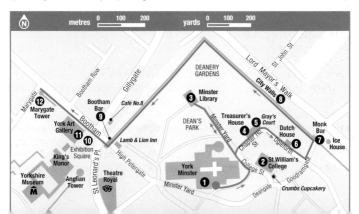

Ⓕ Hidden Minster

Every couple of months from March to November, the Minster offers evening tours of parts of the cathedral not usually accessible to the public. Tours include the West End and Bell Towers, the Chapter House Roof and Mason's Loft. To book, call 01904 557217 or visit www.boxoffice.yorkminster.org (charge).

Above: the Minster hosts a variety of events through the year.

of Durham, and was seen by some as divine retribution (others preferred to blame a UFO). The fire raged for over three hours, causing damage to the famous Rose Window, as well as the roof. It cost £2.25 million to carry out all the repairs. The restored transept was finally rededicated by the Queen in 1988. Major restoration work was also carried out between 1967 and 1972 when cracks were found in the Central Tower and other parts of the cathedral were found to be unstable. Repairs involved giving the tower new steel-reinforced concrete 'feet', which can be seen in the Undercroft.

Above: The Five Sisters' Window at the North Transept in York Minster.

This is still a living church, and regular pauses for prayer are announced over a speaker system. It is also the site for the enthronement of the Archbishop of York. The current Archbishop, John Sentamu, enthroned in November 2005, became the first black archbishop in the Church of England.

Visitors enter via ticket barriers in the South Transept. Anger at the introduction of an entry fee made it all the way to Parliament, where one MP described the imposition as 'tacky'. Nevertheless, claimed Church officials, the money for ongoing restorations must be found somewhere, especially as the Minster costs £20,000 a day to maintain.

Navigating the Minster

Begin your tour in the **Nave Ⓐ** to the west (left as you enter). The main body of the Minster is Decorated Gothic in style and was completed in the 1350s. The 14th-century **West Window Ⓑ** painted in 1338 has become known as the 'Heart of Yorkshire' because of the heart shape in the ornate tracery. The stonework became badly eroded and was replaced and rededicated in 1989. Beneath the window you can see a statue of St Peter, the patron saint of York.

Looking upwards, the shields in the arches of the Nave are the arms of nobles who fought with Edward I and Edward II against the Scots in the 14th

Above: the exquisite octagonal dome inside the Chapter House.

century. The central line of bosses on the roof vaulting portrays scenes from the life of Christ, with one exception. Victorian craftsmen, when called upon to restore the Nave after the fire of 1840, replaced the traditional image of the Virgin Mary breastfeeding baby Jesus with one in which he is being bottle-fed, leaving the Holy Virgin's modesty safely covered. All the other bosses are exact replicas of their medieval versions. The **Dragon's Head C** peeping out from the upper gallery is a crane probably used to lift a font cover. To the right of the Nave is the **Jesse Window D**, a 1310 version of Jesus's family tree, with the Saviour at the top and his ancestor Jesse of Bethlehem at the bottom.

North Transept

The **North Transept E** in Early English style is dominated by the **Five Sisters' Window F** (1260), the oldest complete window in the Minster, which is made of green and grey 'grisaille' glass – clear glass etched with fine black lines and set in geometric patterns. It contains more than 100,000 pieces of glass. The **Astronomical Clock G** is a memorial to 18,000 airmen who lost their lives in World War II while flying from airfields in northern England. One face

shows the position of the stars by which the crews were able to navigate at night. At the nearby **Hindley Clock H**, Gog and Magog, mythical giants associated in legend with the founding of the City of London, strike the hours and quarters. They were made in the 16th century.

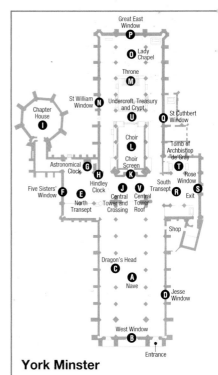

York Minster

Above: choir practice in York Minster.

Chapter House

Located off the corner of the Transept, the **Chapter House** dates back to the 13th century, and is regarded as the architectural wonder of its age. The beautiful domed roof of the octagonal building is not supported by a central pillar. Around the walls are canopied stalls with some of the world's finest medieval carvings, many of them rather cheeky. Look for the man getting rather too close to a ram for decency; at a diagonal, on the other side of the room, a figure wears a carved blindfold, which prevents him from viewing this unedifying sight. Look too for carvings of the Green Man – a pagan figure associated with fertility. The titles in the arched seats denote members of the College of Canons, which meets to decide important issues regarding the Minster.

Choir

The **Central Tower and Crossing** is perpendicular in style, with the ceiling's central carving depicting St Peter and St Paul. The **Choir Screen** is decorated with the statues of 15 kings of England from William I

to Henry VI, all edged with gold and against a scarlet background.

The **Choir** is the focal point of worship in the Minster where daily services are held. It was originally built to prevent 'unprepared' laity from seeing the mass. The ornate stalls are copies of those destroyed in the fire started

Below: the intricate Choir Screen.

Above: the Rose Window honours the end of the Wars of the Roses.

by Jonathan Martin. It is from here that evensong is sung most days. To the right is the Archbishop's **Throne** **M**, or *cathedra*. Found only in a cathedral, as the name suggests, this is the symbol of the Archbishop's authority. Leaving the choir by the left exit, there is the **St William Window** (1422) **N**, showing scenes from the life of Archbishop William Fitzherbert (d. 1154), whose shrine stood near the High Altar until the Reformation.

The **Lady Chapel** **O** in the east end is often used for Holy Communion services. The **Great East Window** **P** above it contains the world's largest area of medieval stained glass in a single window and stands 76ft (23m) high and 32ft (10m) wide. In 1405 a Coventry glazier, John Thornton, started work on the window and completed the task in the contract-agreed three years. He received four shillings a week and £10 on completion. The whole of the east facade is now undergoing restoration. The impressive new attraction, **The Orb** (open until 2016), is housed here, an elliptical treasure house of stained glass from the superb

East Window. Each panel is being meticulously removed and conserved and visitors will be able to see them up close before they are replaced. Four panels will be on permanent show, with a fifth being changed each month revealing the wonderful work of John Thornton, who has often been overlooked as a world-class artist in stained glass. Flanking The Orb are interactive exhibitions relating to the restoration.

On the south side of the choir, the **St Cuthbert Window** (1435) **Q** shows scenes from the saint's life.

South Transept

The **South Transept** **R** was restored after the fire in 1984, and the new ceiling has become a major attraction. Mirrored tables save the neck muscles when examining the superbly carved and decorated new ceiling bosses. All but six of the original carvings were destroyed in the fire.

Spot the Mouse

Sharp young eyes will love searching for the carved wooden mouse on the wooden stalls in the Lady Chapel. It was the trademark of Robert Thompson, the 'Mouseman' carver who came from nearby Kilburn and is still used by the craftsmen at the Mouseman Centre today *(see p.108)*.

Above: master craftsman Robert 'The Mouseman' Thompson at work.

Above: pretty St William's College.

Among the 68 new carvings depicting significant events of the 20th century are six designed by winners of a competition held by children's television programme *Blue Peter*.

Below: mausoleum of William Thomson, archbishop from 1862 to 1890.

The **Rose Window** ⑤ narrowly escaped destruction in the 1984 fire but had to be dismantled and strengthened before being replaced. The red and white roses in the design commemorate the ending of the Wars of the Roses with the wedding in 1486 of King Henry VII and Elizabeth of York – a wedding which united the warring Royal Houses of York and Lancaster and also marked the beginning of the Tudor dynasty.

Against the east wall of the south transept is the **Tomb of Archbishop de Gray** ⑥. Much of the present Minster was of his vision and design. During restoration of his tomb a painting of him was discovered on the coffin lid beneath his marble effigy.

Entrance to the **Undercroft, Treasury and Crypt** ⑪ is via a staircase in the South Transept (charge, wheelchair access via lift). This is now home to the exhibition Revealing York Minster, which opened in summer 2013. The space has been transformed and tells the story of the York Minster site over the last 2,000 years from Roman times to the present day. Archaeological finds recovered during work in the Undercroft are displayed for the first time. State-of-the-art displays and interactives bring the York Minster story to life.

The re-displayed Treasury has a glittering collection of silver plate, including the 11th-century Horn of Ulph, a gift from a Viking thane, and a 13th-century Heart Casket which probably belonged to a crusader. The mysterious York Virgin was found after the fire in 1829 and could date back to the 10th century and be the only remaining fragment of the Saxon Minster.

There are 275 spiralling stone steps to the top of the **Central Tower Roof** Ⓥ (charge). The view is magnificent, but the climb can be claustrophobic and is not advisable for the unfit.

MINSTER LIBRARY AND TREASURER'S HOUSE

Leave the cathedral via the gift shop and follow the path alongside the building to the left, which is known as Queen's Path since Queen Elizabeth II took this route to the Treasurer's House after distributing the Royal Maundy money in 1972.

St William's College

Ahead is the half-timbered **St William's College** ❷. The college now provides an attractive venue for small intimate dinners, banquets and wedding receptions, as well as a conference and exhibition facility.

St William's was constructed between 1465 and 1467 as the home of chantry priests – priests who said mass in the cathedral for those who had given endowments to the chantry. It is named after St William of York, a 12th-century Archbishop who is buried in the Minster. With the Dissolution of the Monasteries in 1536–9, the priests were ordered out and the building passed into private hands, most notably those of Charles I; he set up a printing press here in 1641, firing

Ⓕ Stained Glass

As the Minster slowly took its present form, York became a major centre for glass painting. The whole history of English stained glass, from the 12th century onwards, can be seen within the cathedral. And the medieval artists were not overawed by their subject matter – there was always a place for humour despite the seriousness of the biblical stories they were illustrating. In one window there is a monkey doctor tossing a urine bottle in the air; in the West Window a Nativity scene has a serenely smiling cow.

Amazingly, most of the glass survived the Civil War. The city was put under siege by Roundheads, who didn't care for the 'idolatrous imagery' of stained glass. However, a fellow Yorkshireman, Sir Ferdinando Fairfax, was put in charge. Instead of destroying the windows, he protected them, and saved a glowing tradition of stained glass for us to enjoy today.

Above: York Minster is a treasure trove of stained glass.

F Thou Shalt …

The Minster Library is home to a rare copy of the Wicked Bible. Printed in 1631, this got its name from the fact that the printer omitted to put in the word 'not' in the Commandment 'Though Shalt Not Commit Adultery'. Most of the books were burned on the orders of the Church, but a few managed to survive. Whether the printer's error was deliberate or not is not recorded.

12 ¶ * Honour thy father and thy mo-
þy dayes may bee long vpon the land
ORD thy God giueth thee.
13 * Thou fhalt not kill.
14 Thou fhalt commit adultery.
15 Thou fhalt not fteale.
16 Thou fhalt not beare falfe witne
hy neighbour
17 * Thou fhalt not couet thy neighbo
ou fhalt not couet thy neighbours wif

Above: the famous Commandment 'Thou Shalt Commit Adultery'.

Minster Library

Turn right on leaving St William's and walk along the northern side of the Minster and its Chapter House into **Dean's Park** to see the **Minster Library ③** (Mon–Fri 9am–5pm; visitors must deposit coats and bags in lockers on entry). This is housed in the former 13th-century chapel of the Archbishop's Palace which once covered this area.

The Library – the largest cathedral library in the country – welcomes visitors and offers far more than the theological titles you might expect, with plenty of new titles and an extensive collection of books on Yorkshire history. The original core of the library came from the books of Archbishop Matthew, who died in 1628, supplemented by later donations of books and manuscripts. An extension in 1998 allowed space for a modern reading room, which overlooks the Dean's garden, and conservation space for older documents such as the library's 115 items that date back to before 1500.

One of the jewels of the library is a breviary (prayer book) that belonged to Catherine of Aragon. There's also a fascinating collection of around

off 'paper bullets' in his propaganda war against Parliament. In 1906 it was sold back to the Church and became the meeting place for the bishops and clergy of the Northern Province in the Convocation of York until 1959.

Below: the Treasurer's House is fronted by an attractive formal sunken garden.

Above: built in Roman times, the City Walls have been added to over time.

1,000 theatre playbills, dating from the 1760s to the 1840s. The first 18th-century theatre in York, before the Theatre Royal, was sited close to this building. If you'd like to view special items like this, they must be pre-booked (tel: 0844 939 0021, ID and registration required for all Special Collections). Near the library is the only other remnant of the Archbishop's Palace – the arcading now called the Kohima Memorial.

Treasurer's House

Return by the same route, looking through a gateway into the walled garden of the **Treasurer's House** ❹ (tel: 01904 624247; www.national trust.org.uk; Mar–Oct Sat–Thu 11am–4.30pm, mid–end Feb–Nov 11am–3pm; charge, but garden, tea room and gallery are free).

Built on the site of a property used by a medieval Minster treasurer, this historic gem has passed through many hands over the years and has had any number of changes and additions. It was from here that John Goodricke, the 18th-century astronomer, made his observations. Francis William Green, a Wakefield engineer, exten-

sively restored the house between 1897 and 1900 and filled it with the antique furniture, paintings and ceramics which are on view today. Left empty and untouched for 80 years, the house provides a fascinating glimpse into a bygone era. The National Trust took over the house in 1930, including its cohort of ghosts. They were seen, it is claimed, by a workman doing repairs in the cellar. Roman legionairies marched through one wall and out through the other, but all of them cut off at the knees; a Roman road runs a few feet below the cellar floor.

From the Treasurer's House turn left into cobbled Chapter House Street, where the cottages have overhanging upper storeys. **Gray's Court** ❺ (www.grayscourtyork.com), tucked away in a cobbled courtyard, was the residence of the Treasurers of York Minster from the 11th to the 16th century. It then became the property of Jane Seymour's brother, and in later years was part of a local college. Now a hotel, it has a stunning long gallery lined with Jacobean wood panelling, which is used as a café (see p.26).

Proceed into Ogleforth, probably named after a Dane called Ugel. At

after the Great Fire of London is thought to have prompted this type of fire-resistant construction, and a lack of local knowledge about small-scale brick-building could have forced craftsmen into borrowing a Dutch pattern.

CITY WALLS

Continue into Goodramgate all the way to **Monk Bar** ❼ and on to the **City Walls** ❽. The bar or gateway has four storeys and dates from the 14th century; its external face is adorned with the coat of arms of the Plantagenets.

In the 16th century the rooms were used as a prison. It's now the rather grim **Richard III Museum** (www.richardiiimuseum.co.uk; Mar–Oct 9am–5pm, Nov–Feb 9.30am–4pm; charge), offering visitors the chance to be the Jury at his trial. In the upper room, said to have been added to Monk Bar by Richard III in 1484, visitors can relive the executions he ordered, and view a tiny prison cell.

Outside the ramparts runs a deep ditch – all that remains of a moat that once defended the city. In the springtime the grass banks are speckled with daffodils, but this particular area was not always so pleasant. The Canons of York Minster had their priv-

Above: the four-storeyed Monk Bar is the northeastern entrance to the city.

No. 13 is **Cromwell House**, built in about 1700. Opposite and isolated by the demolition of surrounding property is the curious brick-built **Dutch House** ❻, erected in 1660. Fear of fire among half-timbered structures

---

ⓥ View from the City Walls

The City Walls offer a panoramic view of the city looking across pantiled roofs and gardens to the cathedral and over the Georgian homes around it. You can see the gardens of Gray's Court, where the Royalists held their Civil War battle conferences, and peep into the Dean's garden behind the Minster. Much of this area was occupied by the 12th- and 13th-century Archbishop's Palace, only fragments of which remain.

Above: view from the Walls, the Minster towers looming in the distance.

Above: nudes painter William Etty (1787–1849) was born in York.

ies along these banks, and the city's butchers tossed their offal over the walls into the water. Records from the 15th century describe plagues of flies and vermin and a 'great corruption and horrible and pernicious air'.

Bootham Bar

The wall does a sharp right-angled turn and then runs in a southwesterly direction behind houses in Gillygate. Leave the wall at **Bootham Bar ⑨**, the oldest of the four city gateways, which stands on the site of one of the entrances to the Roman city, Eboracum. It has its portcullis permanently lifted and provides an archer's view through the arrow slits of High Petergate and Bootham.

The view outwards was once straight into the vast Forest of Galtres. Armed guards waited in the bar to act as guides through the dangerous woods and to protect travellers from packs of wolves. Traitors' heads were spiked here – including those of three who were opposed to the Restoration of Charles II. The bar's barbican was removed in the 1830s and the gateway itself was only saved from demolition after strong public protests.

YORK ART GALLERY

Descend into **Exhibition Square ⑩** with its attractive fountain and statue of William Etty, York's most famous artist. He was much abused in his lifetime for his paintings of nudes, but his work dominates the English paintings in the **York Art Gallery ⑪** (www. yorkartgallery.org.uk; closed for redevelopment until Easter 2015). The gallery also has many Old Masters, including the F.D. Lycett Green collection of European art which he donated in 1955. Especially noteworthy are works by two British war artists, Paul Nash (1889–1946) and L.S. Lowry (1887–1976).

During the closure of the gallery, exhibitions drawn from the collec-

Below: York Art Gallery.

Above: make sure to try some real Yorkshire Wensleydale cheese, Wallace and Gromit's favourite!

tions can be found at St. Mary's (see p.45) and the Yorkshire Museum (see p.70). The improved gallery will have 60 per cent more display space, new exhibition areas and a new centre for British Studio Ceramics, plus an entrance at the rear leading into a newly opened-up section of the Museum Gardens.

From Exhibition Square you can see the jagged end of the defensive wall of St Mary's Abbey, torn down at this point in the early 19th century to make way for a new road into the city. It continues up Bootham, where houses have been built against it, to **Marygate Tower** ⑫. This was blown up by the Parliamentarians during the Civil War. They burst in only to be thrown out with heavy losses.

The wall turns at this point and goes down to the river, enclosing the Museum Gardens (see p.69).

ⓔ Eating Out

Café No 8
8 Gillygate; tel: 01904 653074; www. cafeno8.co.uk; Mon–Fri noon–10pm, Sat–Sun 10am–10pm.
Just across the road from Exhibition Square, this cosy daytime café transforms into a lively bistro by night. The inventive dishes include such interesting plates as Yorkshire lamb cooked two ways with North African spices. An excellent value breakfast and brunch is served at weekends, plus special weekday menus. ££

Crumbs Cupcakery
10 College Street; tel: 01904 638282; www.crumbscupcakery.co.uk; Mon–Sat 10am–5pm, Sun 11am–4pm.
Probably the cutest tearoom in town, close to the east end of the Minster. Drink your tea from dainty floral china and enjoy the scrumptious flavours of the myriad of cupcakes on offer; they even do gluten-free ones. There are plenty of other cakes to choose from, too. Eat inside or out, it's a delight. £

Lamb and Lion
2–4 High Petergate; tel: 01904 654 112; www.lambandlionyork.com; food served Mon–Sat noon–8.30pm, Sun noon–6pm.
Nestling in the shadows of the medieval gate of Bootham Bar, and with great views of York Minster, the Lamb and Lion offers classic British pub fare alongside some innovative dishes. Cosy in winter with open fires, and with a beer garden to relish in summer. ££

Gray's Court
Chapter House Street; tel: 01904 612613; www.grayscourtyork.com; daily 9am–5pm.
Sit in squashy sofas in the stunning oak-panelled gallery of this historic house and enjoy a light lunch like a beef and horseradish sandwich, or a delicious Yorkshire rarebit. You can also have afternoon tea with scones and cream. In the summer, you can also sit in the garden. £

Tour 2

Shopping Streets

This half-day tour of some 1½ miles (2.4 km) takes in York's main shopping streets, its administrative headquarters, the centre of the old coaching trade and some ancient churches

Highlights

- Stonegate
- Assembly Rooms
- Mansion House
- Guildhall
- St Martin-le-Grand Church
- All Saints Church
- Parliament Street

Above: shopping on Stonegate is a rewarding experience.

Even in Roman times, Stonegate was a bustling street in York, though it was called Via Praetoria in those days. It's the most popular shopping street in the city today, but still redolent with history. The atmospheric medieval alleyways that lead off it, called snickleways or ginnels,

are particularly rewarding. One takes you to a remnant of a Norman house, while others lead to antique inns. This walk also introduces you to several of the city's churches – overshadowed by the Minster, but still full of interest.

BOOTHAM BAR

Bootham Bar stands on the western entrance to Roman York, the Prima Porta Dextra. High Petergate heads for the centre of town following the line of the old Roman Via Principia. The street was described as one of 'squalor and congestion' in early medieval times, with booths narrowing the thoroughfare. Today

Above: Ye Old Starre Inne sign.

it is smart and attractive but still narrow until it suddenly opens out to an imposing view of the cathedral's twin-towered West Front. When Charles I visited the city the West Front was obscured by a row of cottages and there were houses built along the west and south side of the cathedral, some actually leaning against it. The king protested but it was not until 1702, when the last of the leases expired, that the Minster authorities had them pulled down. In the 19th century the narrow Lop Lane was widened to become Duncombe Place, opening out the present fine view of the cathedral.

St Michael-le-Belfry ❶ gets its name either from the nearby belfry of the Minster, or the bell tower of an earlier church that stood on this site. It has in its register the christening of one Guy Fawkes, son of Edward Fawkes, 16 April 1570 – the man who tried to blow up Parliament on 5 November 1605. Guy's family lived in Stonegate and he attended St Peter's School in Bootham, York. Guy was caught in a cellar beneath Parliament with gunpowder and matches, tortured and eventually hanged, drawn and quartered at Westminster.

A passage in the life of St John of Beverley suggests a very early founda-

tion date for St Michael's, and there might have been a Saxon church on this site. The present church was built between 1525 and 1537, but some original glass survives, such as the East Window which dates to 1330.

At the end of **High Petergate**, at Minster Gates looking towards the South Door of the cathedral, is **Minerva**, goddess of wisdom, leaning on a pile of books in an elegant carving above a corner shop. This is a legacy of a time when this part of the city was dominated by the book trade.

Above: High Petergate with Bootham Bar.

STONEGATE

At this point turn right into **Stonegate** ❷, the finest street in York. The former 15th- and 16th-century houses have been converted into high-quality shops set behind elegant Victorian and Georgian shop facades. Again the Romans got here first – it was their Via Praetoria. During excavation work on the street below the present surface the grooves of chariot wheels were found. The present name means 'stone paved', but this was also the route taken by the Minster masons when hauling their stone to the cathedral site from the river.

A doorway labelled Stonegate Gallery (52A) on the right leads to the remains of the oldest house in the city, now just two walls of a small courtyard. The **Norman House** was built about 1180 and is thought to have been used by the clergy.

A large sign has hung across the street since 1753 pointing down an alleyway to **Ye Olde Starre Inne**, set in its own courtyard and mentioned by name in a Civil War pamphlet of 1644. It was apparently used as a hospital and mortuary. It's said to be the oldest inn in York and, like many inns in the city, is reputedly haunted: in this case by an old lady and two black cats. Nearby is Little Bettys Café – all wooden beams and cosy fires in winter. Its fine cakes and gourmet coffees are the sophisticate's answer to the morning after the night before.

Coffee Yard

Leading off Stonegate to the left is **Coffee Yard**, so called since the coffee houses became popular meeting places in the city. The Irish author Laurence Sterne was a frequent visitor to what he called these 'chit chat' clubs. He 'flirted' with Kitty, a professional singer who lived in the street, and the first edition of his book *Tristram Shandy* was published in 1759 by John Hinxmana, a bookseller in Stonegate. The city's first newspaper was printed here too, which explains the carved red printer's devil at the entrance to Coffee Yard (the 'devils' were the young boys who had to carry the hot metal type).

Ⓢ Stonegate Fashion

Stonegate is a shopping mecca. You'll find branches of high-street favourites Jigsaw and Whistles, as well as White Stuff. Fashionistas with more cash should head just around the corner, to Blake Street, where they'll find the Van Mildert boutique featuring designers such as Vivienne Westwood and Paul Smith.

Above: elegant Stonegate.

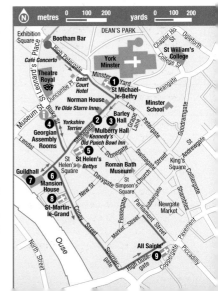

BARLEY HALL

Down the yard is **Barley Hall** ❸ (www.barleyhall.org.uk; Easter–Oct daily 10am–5pm, Nov–Mar 10–4pm; charge). Originally built around 1360 as a townhouse for a priory, the building was altered and extended over the years. In the 15th century it became the home of Alderman William Snawsell, a goldsmith and Lord Mayor of York. In the 1990s archaeologists discovered the remains of the original floor of the great hall, as well as an exterior stairway.

His house has been refurbished by the Barley Hall Trust and is filled with furniture and fittings made by modern craftsmen to recreate the life of a merchant's house. Many of the exhibits are hands-on, and special events, such as Viking markets and medieval fairs, are held throughout the year. Barley Hall also has a programme of exhibitions which aim to give visitors an insight into the lives of former inhabitants of York.

Among the shops in Stonegate is **Mulberry Hall**, a 15th-century bishop's townhouse now selling a range of homeware, crystal and fine china, and serving tea and coffee upstairs. Outside No. 32 is a second reference to Guy Fawkes – the rebel's parents are believed to have lived 'hereabouts'. On a 17th-century, half-timbered shop corner leading into Little Stonegate you can admire a carving of a **topless angel** taken from the prow of a ship. Frequently battered by lorries before the days of pedestrianisation, she has been restored and now faces a more tranquil future.

Nestling among the shops is another historic pub, the 17th-century **Old Punch Bowl Inn**. It was here that members of the Gimcrack Club held their annual lunches, with the winner of the Gimcrack Stakes on Knavesmire having to provide three dozen bottles of champagne for the festivities. The Stakes are still run and the Club meets annually, but these days at the racecourse.

ASSEMBLY ROOMS

Continue down Stonegate to the entrance of St Helen's Square and turn right into Blake Street.

Below: medieval York uncovered at Barley Hall.

Above: Mulberry Hall specialises in fine china and crystal.

On the left you'll find the **Georgian Assembly Rooms**  – a sort of Georgian dance hall. This was the place for fashionable assemblies and balls even though Sarah, Duchess of Marlborough, complained that the space between the pillars was too narrow for her hooped skirts. The building was designed by Richard Boyle, the Third Earl of Burlington, in 1730 and features amongst one of the earliest neoclassical buildings in Europe.

Burlington's hall has been likened to an Egyptian temple with the roof supported by double rows of pillars, 52 in all, decorated with painted yellow and brown marbling and topped by Corinthian-style capitals picked out in gold, green and purple. Burlington's brief was to provide a dancing room not less than 90ft (27m) long and ancillary rooms for cards and refreshments. His design was extremely influential, and the Rooms were hailed as his masterpiece. The cost was borne by public subscription, and the Rooms were ready for the race week of August 1732, although not entirely complete until 1735.

Royalty, nobility and famous beauties patronised the dances – the King of Denmark in 1768 and the Duke of York in 1761, as well as the northern aristocracy. But towards the end of the century the fashion for balls and assemblies waned and the building struggled to find a continuous use.

Ⓕ Café Society

Bettys is a real Yorkshire institution. The first Bettys was opened in 1919 in Harrogate by Frederick Belmont, a Swiss confectioner. The story goes that he had intended to go the south coast of England, but got on the wrong train in London and ended up in Yorkshire – liking it so much that he stayed. The first café was a great success, and in the 1930s he opened a tea room in York, designed in the Art Deco style featured on the *Queen Mary*. There's still a Swiss influence on the menus today, with dishes like Swiss rosti and Alpine macaroni joining the Yorkshire fat rascals and buttered pikelets (large crumpets).

Above: delightful macaroons at Bettys, Yorkshire's number one café.

Above: once a dancing hall to the Georgian upper class, the Assembly Rooms now welcome pizza-lovers from all walks of life.

The 1951 Festival of Britain saw it restored and used for dances, including a Georgian Ball attended by descendants of the families who had paid the original subscriptions. It remained in irregular use for social functions until it took its current, more prosaic role, as home to a chain pizzeria with a far less grand dress code.

Return down Blake Street and into St Helen's Square overlooked by the Mansion House and more fashionable tea rooms. One of them, **Bettys** (see box p.31 and review p.39), with a downstairs bar, was a favourite meeting place for off-duty American and Canadian World War II flyers from the nearby bomber airfields. The mirror on which many scratched their names has been preserved.

ST HELEN'S CHURCH

Tucked in the corner of the square opposite stands **St Helen's Church** ❺, where the Lord Mayor and corporation attend Harvest Thanksgiving every year.

It is convenient for the Mansion House across the square and took over as the city civic church when St Martin's in Coney Street was destroyed in an air raid in 1942. St Helen's narrowly escaped destruc-

Above: St Helen's Church dates back to the 11th century, but was rebuilt in the 16th century.

tion itself in 1552 when it was sold off by the corporation and partly demolished. A local action group was formed and parishioners successfully protested that its loss from the square 'defaced and deformed' the city. It was rebuilt under Crown patronage.

The church has ancient origins, dating back to the early 11th century. Inside you can still see the 12th-century font. Glass-painters associated with the Minster lived in this area and have the **coat of arms** of their guild in the west window of the south aisle.

Concerts and recitals are frequently held in the church, which has the unusual distinction of holding a weekly Sunday service at 11am in Mandarin for the local Chinese community.

Davygate

The church lies at the entrance to Davygate, a name taken from Davy Hall, now demolished, which comes in turn from David the Lardener. His family, which can be traced back as far as the early 12th century, inherited the responsibility for keeping the king's larder at York stocked with food, including game, and domestic animals. In return he received land, rights and privileges which the family duly exercised for more than 200 years. But they ended up in court when there were mutterings about extortion, and

citizens questioned the family's right to take tolls in cash and kind from every food shop in the city.

MANSION HOUSE

At the far side of the square the **Mansion House** ❻ (tours Mar–Dec Fri and Sat at 11am, 12.30 and 2pm, no bookings necessary; charge) is the residence of the city's Lord Mayor during his or her term of office as First Citizen. The house was completed in 1730, 10 years before London's Lord Mayor had his Mansion House. It was lovingly restored by York Civic Trust in 1998. The City Arms adorn the pediment, and in summer, with the window boxes in flower and with its ornate black and gilded railings and lamp-posts sparkling, the building looks as pretty as a doll's house.

Inside the building you can admire the fine state rooms, as well as a superb collection of gold and silver civic plate and regalia including a 15th-century sword which belonged to the Holy Roman Emperor Sigismund.

An ermine-trimmed scarlet Cap of Maintenance was presented to the city by Richard II with the privilege of wearing it before royalty. New caps were bought in 1445 and 1580, and this last cap is still in existence. The latest cap, acquired in 1915, is worn

Ⓚ A Silver Throne

Younger children on a tour of the Mansion House should be entertained to hear about the building's fine silver chamber pot. It was apparently used by George IV, thereby bestowing on it a regal seal of approval. This sparkling convenience is now placed in front of the Lord Mayor when he presides at private dinners.

Above: George IV minus chamber pot.

Above: Mansion House – pretty as a doll's house.

by the current Lord Mayor's attendant on civic occasions.

There is also a Great Mace dated 1657 (at one time the Lord Mayor had six mace bearers) and a gold chain of office made in 1647.

GUILDHALL

Now follow the arched passageway alongside the Mansion House to arrive at the **Guildhall** ❼ (tel: 01904 551027; open on public occasions only, or by appointment). Note the hooks in the ceiling under the archway, which were used to hang game and meat, as a cool larder for the First Citizen's house next door. Underneath the whole complex and reached through an iron gateway (in the wall on the right), a damp passageway runs down to a small quay on the Ouse. It was much used in times when transport by water was safer than by road, and indeed one particularly enterprising Lord Mayor revived its use in recent times. He kept a skiff in the passageway so that he could take a regular row on the river.

The Guildhall at the bottom of the courtyard was first mentioned in 1256

but rebuilt and enlarged in the 15th century. The large **Common Hall** is a replica: the original building was destroyed in an air raid in 1942. Pillars, each made from a single oak tree, support an arch-braced roof with decorated bosses. A magnificent modern stained-glass west window was added during rebuilding. Designed by York artist Harry Harvey, it continues the city's long tradition of glass-painting showing scenes and characters from

Above: the Guildhall's Common Hall.

Above: retail therapy.

York's past. The hall is now used for a variety of exhibitions and meetings, and its future use is under review

It was once used as a Court of Justice. One infamous trial that took place here was that of Margaret Clitherow in 1586, during the Catholic persecutions of Elizabeth I's reign. She was found guilty of keeping items for the celebration of mass in a secret room and crushed to death in punishment. Her stepfather, then Lord Mayor, was one of those who sat in judgement on her.

Off the main hall is Committee Room No. 1, where in 1647, £200,000 in silver was solemnly counted out onto a table – payment from the Parliamentarians to the Scots as a reward for handing over Charles I who had escaped to Scotland. The king was eventually executed in 1649. If staff are available they will show you the two secret panels that conceal passageways – one leads onto the roof, another out to the river.

Since 1810 the city's business has been conducted from here using an upstairs council chamber rich with Victorian carved oak seating and desks, richly adorned walls and windows overlooking the river.

CONEY STREET

Turn along **Coney Street** (a corruption of the Danish for King's Street) and into the city's busy main shopping area. Most of the original properties have been destroyed and there is little to see of old Coney Street, but much to find in the history books. Where tradition has perished, modern commerce has thrived, and this is now one of York's most popular shopping streets.

Ⓖ An Ouse Cruise

Coney Street runs parallel to the River Ouse, which runs through the heart of the walled city. The river is utilised for a variety of city tours, both daytime and early evening. Instead of driving out to a country pub, you could join a lunch or dinner cruise to the waterside Ship Inn at the pretty village of Acaster Malbis. When you reach the inn, you disembark for 1½ hours, plenty of time to enjoy a meal. They operate from April to the end of September (tel. 01904 628324, www.yorkboat.co.uk).

Above: river cruises depart from King's Staith and Lendal Bridge.

Above: the sculpture by Frank Roper (1967) was designed as a reredos for the altar; it depicts the Last Supper, in aluminium covered with gold paint.

St-Martin-le-Grand

Here, though, is what remains of the church of **St-Martin-le-Grand** ❽ after it was fire-bombed during World War II. Some of the church's stained glass was blown out and sank into the tar of the road which had become molten in the inferno. Still proudly 'shooting the sun' with his sextant is the 'Little Admiral', a

Above: the 'Little Admiral' standing proudly on the church clock.

17th-century carved figure above the church clock. The admiral had his coat tails badly singed in the same fire. He returned repaired and re-painted to stand on top of the huge clock which hangs above the pavement on its cast-iron brackets.

St Martin's was one of the city's finest parish churches and it has been partially restored, its open south aisle being dedicated to all those citizens of York who sacrificed their lives in World War II. The restoration work has preserved the former southwest tower and the area around the south door. A large 15th-century stained-glass window, which had been re-moved for safekeeping before the war, has been returned, and there is, moreover, a modern stained-glass window that illustrates the church on fire. Not far away you will find an organ presented to St Martin's by the German government. The church is dedicated to St Martin of Tours, pa-tron saint of soldiers. He's depicted in a window of the church rescuing a hare from hounds.

night stops in inns along the way, and frequent stops to change horses). In 1784 the time was down to three days, and after 1788, express mail coaches were doing the journey far more quickly – eventually getting it down to just one overnight stop. The mail coaches travelled faster partly because they were able to drive through the turnpikes (toll gates) without stopping. The Great North Mail service passed through Coney Street, but in 1820 the city was up in arms after attempts were made to speed up the London to Edinburgh mail by cutting out York. The city protested and kept its fast link 'up to town'.

There is, however, no marker for another famous Coney Street coaching inn, the George, at which Sir John Vanburgh stayed while supervising the building of Castle Howard. Somewhere in this street, too, lived Aaron of York, the greatest of all the 13th-century Anglo-Jewish financiers. He is said to have financed a loan for building the Five Sisters' Window in the Minster before he was cheated by Henry III and reduced to penury.

The old coach trade

A plaque on a wall by the Yorkshire Bank marks the site of the Black Swan Inn and is the only visible clue to what Coney Street once was – the thriving centre for the city's long-distance coach trade. Coaches leaving the two coaching inns in Coney Street in 1658 took four days to reach the capital (there would have been over-

🄵 Bombs on York

York was damaged more than once by wartime bombs. In 1916, during WWI, there were Zeppelin raids on the city. During WWII, the city suffered again, when Baedeker raids by German bombers damaged York railway station. These raids gained their name because targets were chosen for their historic importance through the Baedeker tourist guidebooks. The aim was to destroy morale. 'We shall go out and bomb every building in Britain marked with three stars in the Baedeker Guide,' said Baron Gustav Braun von Sturm, on 24 April 1942. Thankfully York Minster escaped.

Above: squad group photo outside a bunker in York in 1940.

ALL SAINTS CHURCH

Continue past the shops into Spurri-ergate and turn left into High Ouseg-ate to **All Saints Church** ❾, Pave-ment. This church is very ancient, for it was mentioned in the Domesday Book (1086). It has a replica of a 13th-century 'doom' or sanctuary **knocker** on the door showing a bearded sinner being eaten by a lion – a representation of the mouth of hell. A fugitive laying hold of the door knob could claim sanctuary from his pursuers, which he maintained until he came out again.

The church was once thought to be in possession of an extraordinary relic – the platter on which the head of John the Baptist was borne to Herod. It seems to have disappeared around the 14th century. Fortunate perhaps, as John Welsey, who preached here from the pulpit in 1634, would cer-tainly not have approved. Another of the church's claims to fame is the unusual open-top lantern tower. A lantern has hung here since medi-eval times so that travellers passing

Above: the evocative door knob of All Saints Church.

through the nearby dark Forest of Galtres could see in which direction the city lay. The light still shines, but as a war memorial.

The church has been pinched by busy roads. In the 17th century the churchyard to the north and south was taken for street-widening, and in 1782 the chancel was demolished so the market in Pavement could be

Below: Parliament Street has a French air.

made larger. No fewer than 39 Lord Mayors are buried in the church, which still has strong links with the Corporation. The surviving city guilds process in their robes to this church for annual services.

PARLIAMENT STREET

Now turn left into **Parliament Street** past the site locals called the 'splash palace' – a former Victorian public convenience, which was demolished in 2012, opening up the view. Parliament Street has been transformed into a delightful Yorkshire version of a French town square. The area has been paved and planted with plane trees, decorated with a fountain and set out with seats which attract crowds of visitors and locals to watch the street entertainers in the summer. This broad open space was created in 1836 by knocking down old property to allow the overcrowded market in Pavement to expand. The market, however, has since contracted and been moved into Newgate (see p.43).

Ⓔ Eating Out

Bettys
6–8 St Helen's Square; tel: 01904 659142; www.bettys.co.uk; daily 9am–9pm.
Be prepared to queue at Bettys. This genteel café-teashop is now almost as much a part of the tourist trail as the Minster, and few people come to York without enjoying tea and cakes here. Come for a traditional afternoon tea, with dainty sandwiches, scones, cakes and a good strong Yorkshire brew. Or you can try one of their Swiss dishes, such as rosti or Alpine macaroni. Their hearty brunches are popular at weekends. ££

Café Concerto
21 High Petergate; tel: 01904 610478; www.cafeconcerto.biz; daily 8.30–10pm.
Very popular with the locals, this café near the Minster becomes a bistro in the evening. Come during the day for bagels, baguettes, salads and homemade cakes. At night, you'll be served dishes like grilled sea bass, Aberdeen Angus cottage pie, or local pork sausages with mash. ££

DCH – The Restaurant
Duncombe Place; tel: 01904 625082, www.deancourt-york.co.uk; daily 7–9.30pm, Sat–Sun 12.30–2pm; bistro Mon–Sat 9.30am–10pm, Sun 10am–7pm.
This restaurant in the Dean Court Hotel is in a convenient location just beside the Minster. It has a menu that features plenty of top-quality local produce. Main courses include roast venison from Fountains Abbey or breast of local pheasant. There will be options for vegetarians too. For dessert, choose from an iced orange and cranberry soufflé and a good selection of local cheeses. For less formal dining, the hotel also has a bistro/café. £££

Kennedy's
1 Little Stonegate; tel: 01904 620222, www.kennedysbaryork.co.uk; food served daily noon–9.30pm.
This bar-restaurant offers relaxed dining in contemporary surroundings. The food is international, with everything from salmon fishcakes to vegetable Malaysian curry or spare ribs on the menu. There's a separate children's menu, so it's ideal for families. ££

Yorkshire Terrier
10 Stonegate; tel: 01904 676722, www.yorkbrewery.co.uk; food served daily noon–4pm.
This popular pub, on Stonegate, offers good food along with a selection of real ales. Come for good-value pub favourites such as jacket potatoes, fish and chips, or steak and ale pie. On Sundays, between noon and 4pm they serve a traditional Sunday roast – with a rich ale gravy. ££

The Art Scene

There are concerts, musicals and plays to enjoy throughout the year in York – as well as an array of entertaining and diverse annual festivals

York has long had a rich artistic scene, with a theatrical tradition that stretches back to medieval times.

THE MYSTERY PLAYS

Jugglers and tumblers at the great medieval fairs provided locals with their first taste of 'theatre', and their successors, the buskers, are still around today tossing flaming torches in the air and teetering about on unicycles.

But it was a medieval monk at St Mary's Abbey who is thought to have been responsible for putting depth and power into the city's street theatre. He produced the York Cycle of Mystery Plays – with its plot spanning the Creation to the Day of Judgement. With powerful simplicity and earthy humour, the Plays present a stark choice between good and evil – heaven and its angels and hell with its romping, pitchfork-wielding devils. The amateur actors of the city's guilds performed the plays, with pageant wagons acting as mobile stages; these set off each year from Holy Trinity in Micklegate, each guild performing at different stations around the city.

However, the Plays ran into trouble with the Reformation. Disputes arose about some of their theology, and in the streets the holiday spirit occasionally got out of hand. Religious leaders

Festivals

York hosts a variety of festivals through the year. Some of the main ones are:

- **Jorvik Viking Festival** (www.jorvik-viking-centre.co.uk) in February. Celebrates York's Viking heritage with various family-oriented events including lectures, arts and crafts, saga-telling and battle re-enactments.
- **York Literature Festival** (www.yorkliteraturefestival.co.uk) in March. Hosts events throughout York, including theatre, storytelling, workshops, author signings and much more.
- **Early Music Festival** held at the National Centre for Early Music in July (they also have a Christmas Festival).
- **Food and Drink Festival** (www.yorkfoodfestival.com) in September. This is a showcase for Yorkshire food, with stands from farms all over the county. Events take place across the city and include cookery workshops.

THEATRE AND MUSIC

The Theatre Royal was built to entertain the noble – and not so noble – who once crowded into the city for the races, the assizes (public hangings were a popular spectacle) or just to attend the markets. The theatre's most charismatic manager, Tate Wilkinson, realised that it was only the coarser entertainments that made a profit, and the only way he could make money out of Shakespeare was through the 'star' system. People would turn up to watch if Sarah Siddons or John Philip Kemble were performing. But he persisted and succeeded in giving York a prestige approaching that of the London theatres.

Today the Theatre Royal (www.yorktheatreroyal.co.uk) stages ballet, classical concerts, comedy shows and pantomime, while the Grand Opera House (www.grandoperahouseyork.org.uk) hosts popular musicals.

complained of drunken irreverence, and in 1572 they called in all the play books 'for examination' – and kept them. The Plays were not publicly performed again until the Festival of Britain in 1951. Now the pageant wagons roll through the city streets every four years, creating a stunning spectacle. They are next due to be performed in 2014 (the last time was in July 2010). To find out more visit: www.yorkmysteryplays.co.uk.

Above: the red and gilded interior of the Theatre Royal. **Top Left**: York Food and Drink Festival. **Bottom Left**: Pilate and family are cheered by the inhabitants of Jerusalem in a York Mystery Plays performance.

Tour 3

Markets and Museums

This 1½-mile (2.4km) tour starts in the busy heart of the city and takes in the picturesque Shambles and fascinating Jorvik Viking Centre – all in around half a day

A stroll along the Shambles is a 'must' on any trip to York. This much-photographed shopping street was mentioned in the Domesday Book of 1086 and is characterised by its pleasing jumble of timber-framed buildings. The shops may now be firmly aimed at the tourist trade, but the Shambles' charm is undiminished.

Even earlier times are recalled at the ever-popular Jorvik Viking Centre, which manages to make history engaging to all ages, without stinting on accuracy or detail. Children will love it – and are also sure to appreciate the Castle Museum, with its reconstructed Victorian street, which you reach later on this tour. Finish the walk with a drink at the King's Arms pub on the banks of the Ouse.

Highlights

- King's Square
- The Shambles
- Jorvik Viking Centre
- Fairfax House
- Clifford's Tower
- Castle Museum

THE SHAMBLES

King's Square ❶ is the place to be in summer, particularly at lunchtime. Jugglers, acrobats and pavement artists provide some of the best busking entertainment in the north of England. A royal Viking court is thought to be responsible for the name, but the square only came into existence in 1937 when the ancient church of Holy

Left: Newgate Market.

Trinity, King's Court, was pulled down. Old tombstones from the graveyard are set into the square's pavements. The square is also home to the city's newest attraction, York's Chocolate Story *(see p.76)*

The Shambles ❷ starts in the southeast corner of the square and gives an immediate impression of what York must have looked like in the 15th century, but without the squalor and the smells. This is one of the best-preserved and oldest medieval streets in the whole of Europe, although the shop fronts have been restored.

The name Shambles derives from the medieval term for bench or booth, 'shamel', on which goods were sold. It was also called Fleshammels (the street of the butchers), for this is where animals were both slaughtered and butchered. The broad window sills are a legacy of the shelves on which meat was displayed – blood and offal would drain away along channels in the cobbled street.

The half-timbered houses lean inwards and are so close that neighbours could shake hands with each other across the street: living in such close proximity meant that outbreaks of the plague could spread rapidly. The butchers' shops have long gone. Instead there are gift and craft shops and the only odours (all pleasant) come from a pizza restaurant. The old **Butchers' Hall** is at No. 41. At No. 35 there is a shrine to **Margaret Clitherow** – though she probably lived at No. 10. She was a butcher's wife who was pressed to death in 1586 for harbouring Jesuit priests. She was canonised as St Margaret of York in 1970.

Around the Shambles

Three narrow alleyways on the right lead into the **Newgate Market ❸**,

Above: great for souvenir-shopping.

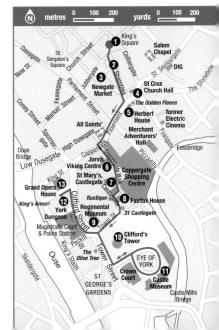

open daily with stalls selling everything from fish to fashions. York's medieval markets were so famous and grew so large that city-centre property had to be demolished to accommodate them (see p.39). It is much more modest now, but Henshelwood's Delicatessen is one of many fine food shops trading here with its tempting array of cheeses, chutneys, oils, olives, pasta and cakes.

At the end of the street on the left is **St Crux Church Hall ④** (there is no saint called Crux – the name means Holy Cross). What was once the finest medieval church in York was declared unsafe and demolished in 1887 and the church hall built from the stones. Inside are some of the memorials from the original church. The hall is used by various charitable groups for fundraising, so between Tuesday and Saturday you might find homemade cakes, books or bric-a-brac for sale.

Pavement – the first paved street in the city – was the main market area, the place for executions and where 'minor' punishments such as whippings and pillorying took place. Overlooking the street is the richly carved **Herbert House ⑤**, the finest black and white half-timbered building in the city, now home to a shoe shop.

Christopher Herbert, Lord Mayor of London, bought a house on this site in 1557, and it was altered and extended over the years. His great-grandson, Sir Thomas Herbert, was born here in 1606 and became a valet to Charles I. It's possible that the king was entertained here on a royal visit to York in 1639. He later attended the king on his way to execution and was given the cloak that Charles I removed from his shoulders on the scaffold.

JORVIK VIKING CENTRE

Continuing along Pavement towards the tower of All Saints, pass the church to your right and then turn left into Coppergate Walk. This was the site of a sweet factory before it became an archaeological dig often visited by British and Scandinavian royalty in the late 1970s. It was here that the wooden house walls and wicker fences of Viking Jorvik were discovered standing shoulder-high. On the spot where they were found (beneath the new shops), the discoveries have been given a new lease of life in the **Jorvik Viking Centre ⑥** (tel: 01904 615505; www.jorvik-viking-centre.co.uk; daily 10am–5pm, 10am–4pm in winter, pre-booking advised during peak periods; charge,

Below: learn all about Viking life at the Jorvik Viking Centre.

Above: Viking craftswoman at work.

joint tickets available with DIG). This highly popular attraction had a £1 million redevelopment in 2010, and takes account of continuing research into the Viking city that was found on the site.

You first enter a room with a glass floor, beneath which you can see some of the original archaeological site, while displays on the walls explain the Viking civilisation. 'Time cars' then whisk visitors back to a reconstructed Viking world which displays the life and smells of the Viking city. Each house stands on the site of an original Viking property, and the ride features animatronic characters based on archaeological evidence from the Coppergate dig. Market craftsmen are at work, and characters chatter at you in old Norse as you pass. Studies of plant and animal remains in the original dig threw new light on the diet and hygiene of the inhabitants of this huge Viking town as they set about the more peaceful occupations of farming and trade (there were plenty of human fleas and lice in their homes, for example). The time-car ride ends in a gallery filled with exhibits of finds and explains archaeological techniques.

A new, reassessed image of the Vikings emerges, but it is the established reputation of rapists and pillagers that probably attracts the crowds. This rough and ready image still dominates Jorvik's Viking Festival held every February (see p.41), which features ferocious battles and have-a-go kids' sword combat – although poetry and crafts also get a look-in.

Next door is **St Mary's, Castlegate** ❼ (free). This predominantly 15th-century building has Saxon origins but was declared redundant in 1958 and was bought by the city council for a nominal five pence in 1972. It has the

---

🄺 Life with the Vikings

At Jorvik there are lots of activities for children, in addition to the journey on the 'dark ride'. They can also see the skeleton of a Viking killed in battle, handle replicas of tools and objects found in the original dig, and use touchscreens to get a more in-depth insight into the daily life of the Vikings in York. They're sure to be fascinated by some of the insalubrious details – such as the fact that remains of human faeces were found in toilet pits.

Above: the skeleton of a Viking swordsman at the Jorvik Centre.

Above: Fairfax House was brought back to grandeur by the York Civic Trust.

tallest spire in York at 154ft (47m) high, and is now used to house an annual site-specific installation and temporary exhibitions from the York Art Gallery.

FAIRFAX HOUSE

Behind St Mary's continue along Castlegate towards Clifford's Tower and on the left is **Fairfax House** ❽ (tel: 01904 655543; www.fairfax house.co.uk; mid-Feb–end Dec, Tue–Sat 10am–5pm, Sun 12.30–4pm; guided tours Mon 11am and 2pm only; charge). One of the finest Georgian houses in England, it was rescued from decay by the York Civic Trust. It was purchased in 1762 as a dowry for Anne Fairfax, the only surviving child of Viscount Fairfax, and it has been refurbished to look very much as it would have in its 18th-century heyday.

The stunning interiors conjure up an elegant, forgotten world and the ceilings are all original. The dining room, for instance, where the Fairfax family entertained, has a table laid with fine silverware and porcelain, while the library contains a stunning walnut long-case clock. The furniture and clocks

were donated by Noel Terry, the great-grandson of the founder of the Terry's confectionery business in York. Items on display upstairs include a fine walnut bureau with secret drawers.

You enter the house through the former **St George's Cinema** – its Greek-style entrance from 1911 is re-

Above: the ascent to Clifford's Tower is rewarded with great views.

the north country under control. The northern English, helped by the Danes, burned down the wooden castle on the mound within a year. Another wooden keep was built during William's 'harrowing of the north', but was burned down again in anti-Jewish riots in 1190. Some 150 Jews took their own lives when they were trapped in the tower by a mob – it's thought that the tower was then set alight to try to erase all trace of the horror. There is a plaque to their memory at the foot of the mound.

The stone tower, completed in 1270, was heavily fortified and then wrecked in 1684 when a fire – some say started deliberately – set off the powder magazine and blew off the roof, leaving the structure as it is today.

The tower's name might well have derived from the powerful Clifford family, hereditary constables in the

garded as a piece of early 20th-century architectural history in its own right. The cinema foyer is now the entrance and gift shop of the house.

In Tower Street is the **Regimental Museum** ❾ of the 4th and 7th Royal Dragoon Guards and the Prince of Wales's Own Regiment of Yorkshire (Mon–Sat 9.30am–4.30pm; charge). The museum has displays of regimental colours, uniforms, medals and models of battles fought all over the world by the two regiments. There are also oil paintings and watercolours, including works by the WWII artist Edward Payne. Contemporary soldiers' clothing is also displayed, as well as modern ration packs, with their vacuum-sealed meals and water purification tablets.

CLIFFORD'S TOWER

The huge mound facing the visitor at the end of Castlegate and topped by **Clifford's Tower** ❿ (tel: 01904 646940; www.english-heritage.org. uk; daily Apr–Sept 10am–6pm, Oct 10am–5pm, Nov–Mar 10am–4pm; charge) was hurriedly thrown up by William the Conqueror two years after the Battle of Hastings to keep

Ⓥ Towering Views

The ramparts of Clifford's Tower offer some great views of the city – and although not as spectacular as those from the tower at York Minster, the climb is less arduous. The views are panoramic, so you have the chance to take striking photographs at various times of day. However, you won't get any summer sunsets, as the tower closes at 6pm.

Above: view from Clifford's Tower.

area, or it could be a reference to Sir Richard Clifford, who was hanged there in 1322 after a failed rebellion.

One of York citizens' earliest attempts at conservation came in 1596 when Robert Redhead, a jailer, began to pull down the tower intending to burn the masonry for lime. He was stopped after petitions to the government claiming that the tower was 'an especial ornament for the beautifying of this city'. There are information panels inside the tower.

YORK CASTLE MUSEUM

Beyond the tower mound can be seen what 18th-century travellers regarded as 'the finest gaol in Britain if not in Europe'. The former Debtors' Prison (with a clock on the roof) and adjoining Female Prison now house the city's **Castle Museum ⑪** (tel: 01904 687687; www.yorkcastlemuseum.org. uk; daily 9.30am–5pm; charge), named after York Castle, which once stood on this site.

The museum is constantly evolving from its original display, which sprang from a collection of 'everyday things'

gathered together by Dr John Kirk, a Pickering country doctor, during his rounds in rural North Yorkshire. He saw a way of life slowly disappearing and was determined to keep mementoes of its passing.

As a result of a recent £1.7 million project much of the original display has been updated and reorganised. You can view more than 400 years of York's past, with social and military history covered on a large scale, together with more intimate and personalised objects. Amongst many fascinating items in the collection is a faded and battered cocoa tin. This was taken to the Antarctic in 1908–9 by Shackleton in his failed attempt to reach the South Pole. It was never used, as Shackleton and his team had to turn back before reaching the Pole. Every period is vividly brought to life, including a tribute to the swinging '60s, complete with mopeds and miniskirts.

Kirkgate

The covered courtyard became the impressive **Kirkgate**, a cobbled street created from original 19th-century

Below: York Castle Museum is one of Britain's leading museums of everyday life, recreating rooms, shops, streets – and even prison cells.

F Dick Turpin

Born in Essex in 1706, Dick Turpin was the son of an innkeeper, but far from the romantic figure of legend. He joined a gang of thieves, then became a highwayman in 1735. He later shot a man and escaped to Yorkshire, with a price on his head. He changed his name to John Palmer, but was soon arrested again for horse-stealing. He was imprisoned in York Castle Prison. His real identity was revealed when he wrote to his brother for help, signing himself John Palmer. His brother wouldn't pay the postage, so the letter was returned to the post office, where it happened to be seen by Turpin's former teacher – who rec-ognised the handwriting. The teacher was asked to travel to York, where he formally identified Turpin. The high-wayman was hanged in 1739 and is buried in St George's churchyard.

Above: the famous highwayman's grave in St George's churchyard.

shop fronts and filled with the samples of Victoriana collected by the doctor. Every shop is now based on a real York business from the period 1870–91. Trades represented include grocer, saddler, taxidermist, draper, pawnbroker and more. Of particular interest is John Saville's chemist shop at the corner of the newly created backstreet, the poverty-stricken Rowntree Snicket, whose occupants used the chemist's skills as they could not afford a doctor.

The museum eventually expanded in 1952 into the Debtors' Prison next door. Turn right when you enter and you'll come to the exhibition, York Castle Prison. It illustrates the harsh conditions that would have been experienced by prisoners in these buildings. Dick Turpin (see box above) was imprisoned here – he was tried at the Assize Courts next door.

Assize Courts
The Assize Courts, which extend like a wing from one side of the Debtors' Prison, were built in the years 1773–7.

The Courts, which were designed by John Carr, have an Ionic pillared entrance and a figure of Justice carrying scales and a spear on the roof. Restoration work revealed that Justice had not always been even-handed – her scales had been balanced with

Below: recreating dishes of times gone by inside Clifford's Tower.

small coins put into the weighing cups. Courts still sit in the two Georgian courtrooms, each set beneath an ornately decorated dome. Apart from Dick Turpin's, the famous trials held here have included such social *causes célèbres* as the Luddites in 1812 and the Peterloo rioters in 1820.

Eye of York

Together with the museum, the buildings constitute three sides of a square. Between them lies a sizeable, circular grassed area called the Eye of York. County elections used to be held here, proclamations were read, and prisoners executed. What so impressed the Georgians was the spaciousness of the exercise yard in front of the Debtors' Prison, where prisoners could walk and talk to friends through the yard railings. A verse scratched on the yard wall is preserved behind glass:

Below: the picturesque setting of the King's Arms pub along the Ouse.

This prison is a house of care, a grave for man alive
A touchstone to try a friend, no place for man to thrive.

The poet was Thomas Smith, aged 28, who was imprisoned here for sheep-stealing and hanged in 1820.

YORK DUNGEON

Retrace your steps back to the entrance and turn right to go down Tower Street and onto Clifford Street. The **York Dungeon** ⑫ (tel: 01904 632599; www.thedungeons.com/york; Feb–Oct daily 10.30am–4.30pm (until 5.30pm Easter and summer school holidays), Nov–Jan 11am–4pm; charge) is the city's own chamber of horrors – complete with blood, groans and mutilations. Dick Turpin, Guy Fawkes, Vikings and witches all feature in this thoroughly ghoulish attraction.

OPERA HOUSE

The nearby **Grand Opera House** ⑬ (www.grandoperahouseyork.org.uk) opened in 1902 as a music hall rival to the Theatre Royal. It was converted from two buildings: an old warehouse and corn exchange by the London theatre architect John Briggs. It 'went dark' in 1956, reopened in 1956 for roller skating, dancing and bingo, and after another period of gloom it is again operating as a theatre, with performances for everything from comedians to musicals. Backstage tours are available in which you learn about the theatre's history, see the dressing rooms and go on stage. To book, call 0844 847 2322 (charge).

Walk down the street on the left to King's Staith where, in summer, picnic tables are set out on the riverbank in front of the King's Arms. This frequently photographed pub often features in the news when floodwater from the Ouse invades its cellars and drinking areas.

Above: the buildings that comprise the Grand Opera House were not originally intended to be a theatre but York's corn exchange and an adjoining warehouse.

🄴 Eating Out

31 Castlegate
31 Castlegate; tel: 01904 621404; www.31castlegate.co.uk; Tue–Sun 11am–3pm, 5.30–9.30pm.
Situated beside Fairfax House, this restaurant offers a diverse menu with dishes that can vary with the seasons. During the day, pop in for salads, filled baguettes, or a homemade burger with bacon and cheese. In the evening, mains might include slow roast free-range belly of pork, pan fried sea bream, or assiette of venison. ££

The Golden Fleece
16 Pavement; tel: 01904 625171; www.thegoldenfleeceyork.co.uk; food served: Mon–Fri noon–3pm, 5–8pm, Sun noon–8pm.
York's oldest and supposedly most haunted pub, it certainly has the old-world wow factor. Stop here for a drink in the beer garden, or a meal cooked using locally sourced ingredients in the cosy dining room. Good wholesome pub fare includes steak and ale pie and fish and chips. Gluten-free meals available. ££

The Olive Tree
10 Tower Street; tel: 01904 624433; www.theolivetreeyork.co.uk; daily noon–2pm and 5.30–10pm.
You get stunning views of Clifford's Tower at this sleek little restaurant, which sits just across the road from the imposing fortification. The food is modern Mediterranean, and local produce is used whenever possible. There are pizzas and pasta dishes, as well as main courses such as char-grilled fillet of salmon or Yorkshire beef. Desserts might include a rich chocolate orange brûlée cheesecake, served with caramel sauce, or panna cotta with strawberries. ££

Rustique
28 Castlegate; tel: 01904 612744; www.rustiqueyork.co.uk; Mon–Sat noon–10pm, Sun noon–9pm.
This cosy restaurant, tucked away on Castlegate, serves delicious French fare. The three-course set menu is good value. Dishes are French favourites such as moules marinière for starters, with mains like pork with apples and French cider, or fillet of beef with truffles. Save some space for dessert and choose from the classic tarte tatin, traditional crème brûlée or an indulgent pot au chocolat. ££

Tour 4

An Aerial View of York's Railway History

This 1³/₄-mile (2.8km) walk takes a couple of hours, starting along the City Walls, looking down on scenes of York's railway past, then returns along the old main road from London

This gentle walk gives you the opportunity to appreciate the beauty of York's riverside setting, taking you over the Ouse for a stroll along the city's superbly preserved walls. You get a reminder of the exuberant optimisim of the Victorian age, with great views of the 19th-century railway station – a cathedral to steam which established a fast link between York and London. There are also reminders of the religiosity of the medieval era, as you pass churches such as All Saints. You could end the walk with a wander along Queen's Staith, which runs right beside the river. Warehouses here have been converted into apartments and hotels.

Highlights

- City Walls
- Micklegate Bar
- St Martin cum Gregory
- St John Micklegate
- Ouse Bridge
- All Saints, North Street

UP THE WALLS

Lendal Bridge was built in 1863 to cope with the extra traffic attracted to the city's first railway station located south of the river inside the bar walls. Previously there had only been a rope ferry at this point. Work began in 1860, but in 1861 the struc-

Left: handsome Lendal Bridge crosses the Ouse.

ture collapsed and several workmen were killed. A new architect was brought in, Thomas Page, designer of Westminster Bridge in London, and a new bridge boasting Gothic-style features opened in 1863. Tolls were imposed until 1894 in order to pay for the cost and compensation to the ferryman.

Lendal Tower ❶, on the north bank and once part of the city's medieval defences, was in 1677 given to a London businessman on a 500-year lease and for a peppercorn rent on condition he supplied piped water to the city within three years. He did so through pipes made of hollowed-out elm tree trunks – each half of the city getting water for three days a week in turn. During assizes and busy race weeks water-carriers were drafted in to supply the whole city. It is now a private residence.

Ⓖ City Walls Walk

York's City Walls make a great walking route. At 2 miles (3.2 km) long, they take around two hours to walk and offer fine views of iconic structures like the Minster – as well as peeks into pretty gardens and courtyards. However, don't think that the Romans or Vikings strolled around the city in this fashion. The walkway was only constructed in Victorian times – allowing ladies and gentlemen to make an elegant promenade.

Above: exploring the City Walls.

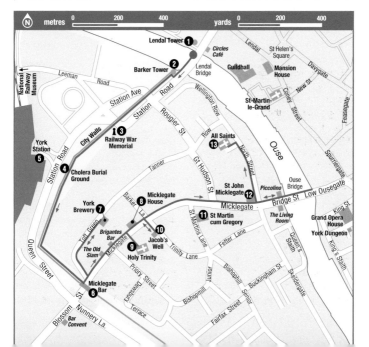

Barker Tower

Cross over the river to where the medieval **City Walls** start again from **Barker Tower** ❷ on the far river-bank. An iron chain once hung between the two towers so that water-borne traders could not avoid tolls. Barker Tower was used as a mortuary in the 19th century for bodies recovered from the river. More recently it has housed a variety of shops and is now a café.

Railway War Memorial

The walls run southwards from here, following the line of the defences which the Romans put around their civil settlement. Walk along the parapet over the top of the busy road leading to the station and below to the left is the white obelisk on the **Railway War Memorial** ❸, commemorating the 2,236 men of the North Eastern Railway who died in WWI. It was designed by Sir Edwin Lutyens, also responsible for

Above: Barker Tower.

the Cenotaph in London. Behind the memorial are the former headquarters offices of the North Eastern Railway, built in 1906. They now house a five-star hotel. Outside the wall is an area of grass, trees and gravestones – the **Cholera Burial Ground** ❹, where 185 victims of an epidemic in 1832 are interred. Superstitious fears of reawakening the disease are said to have preserved the area from development.

Look back along the parapet to enjoy a postcard-perfect view of York Minster across the river. Beyond the city, you can also see one of the city's finest Victorian buildings, the **Royal York**, formerly the Station Hotel.

RAILWAY STATION

Below is York's 'new' **Railway Station** ❺, dating from 1877 and regarded as one of the finest examples of Victorian railway architecture. The plain brick entrance belies the magnificence within – a gracefully curved 'train shed' covering four lines of through traffic with the curved roof supported on iron Corinthian pillars.

The roof arches are pierced with quatrefoil patterns and the spandrels decorated with the Rose of York and the coats of arms of the three companies which amalgamated to form

Below: two towers mark the ends of Lendal Bridge, Barker Tower to the west and Lendal Tower to the east.

the North Eastern Railway in 1853. A £900,000 refurbishment of the entrance area was completed in 1984, giving the outer concourse a more welcoming appearance and adding a decorative old North Eastern Railway semaphore signal. The station is now a listed building.

All railways come to York

York's first railway station was a temporary affair sited outside the medieval wall near where it turns at a right angle. This station was quickly found to be inadequate, so an archway was punched through the city ramparts (which you walk over) and the railway line came under the walls to a purpose-built station inside – an area now occupied by offices. These were the golden days of York's Lord Mayor and railway 'king', George Hudson *(see box below)*, whose proud boast was to 'mak' all railways cum t'York'. The new Lendal Bridge and a new road, George Hudson Street, helped more and more railway passengers to get to his station, but the site was too cramped. The terminus was moved back outside the walls to the 'new' station on its present site.

Above: a masterpiece of Victorian railway architecture.

Although George Hudson fell into disgrace in a shares scandal, York continued to be a geographical and administrative focal point for railways.

Under the wall and earth mound at this point was a railway control room for keeping the region's railways running during WWII. It came into its own when the station was badly bombed during the Baedeker raid on the city in 1942. In the entrance to the station is a restored 19th-century trackside railway signal. It was only taken out of service in 1984.

Ⓕ Changing Faces

Near the railway station, just outside the City Walls, is a statue to George Leeman. A lawyer and politician, Leeman was also a rival of George Hudson, the York 'railway king' who at one time co-owned a third of Britain's railways. He was a major influence in investigating Hudson's shady share dealings – which led to the latter's downfall. Leeman then became chairman of the powerful North Eastern Railway Company. This statue was originally of Hudson, but after his demise the head was replaced with Leeman's. A humiliation indeed.

Above: Leeman's head was superimposed onto Hudson's statue.

MICKLEGATE

Leave the rampart walk at the royal entry point to the city, **Micklegate Bar** . The imposing southern entrance to the city was erected in the 12th–14th centuries, probably over an ancient track from the south leading down to the River Ouse. A succession of kings and queens of England have traditionally entered York here *(see box right)*. Although restored in 1737, the barbican – two protective walls extending in front of the gate – was pulled down in 1839 despite the protests of Sir Walter Scott. His offer to walk from Edinburgh to York if the council would change their minds went unheeded. This was another gateway which was often 'decorated' with spiked heads, most famously that of the Duke of York in 1460 during the Wars of the Roses. Queen Margaret in Shakespeare's *Henry VI Part 3* put the incident succinctly:

Off with his head, and set it on York gates
So York may overlook the town of York.

The last heads to be displayed here were those of Jacobites captured after the Battle of Culloden in 1745. Spectators on these walls in 1644 saw the

disastrous aftermath of the Battle of Marston Moor, when fugitives and wounded royalist survivors clamoured for admission with the Roundheads hot on their heels. Queen Elizabeth II and the Duke of Edinburgh were welcomed here by pageantry and fanfare when they formally sought entry to the city as part of the York's 1,900th anniversary celebrations in 1971. A museum *(see box above)* in the bar portrays the social history of this ancient gate.

A wealthy street

Micklegate was York's most important street – it led to the only bridge in the city over the River Ouse and was part of the long road between London and Edinburgh. Its importance attracted the richer residents of the city and medieval merchants, and leading Georgian businessmen built their townhouses here.

Apart from passing traffic business, Micklegate was close to the quays and the lucrative river trade. Look above today's shop fronts to see the character and quality of what were once fine town residences. In modern times the street has entered local folklore for

---

🄵 Micklegate Bar Museum

Now under the umbrella of the York Archaeological Trust, this museum reveals the history of the city's walls, in its exhibition Ring of Stone. Delve into York's bloody history represented in the Ring of Steel display, featuring Viking invasions, rebellions and civil war. Micklegate Bar was also a home until 1918 and the story of the residents is brought alive in the Life in the Bar exhibition (tel: 01904 615505; www.micklegatebar.com; daily Apr–Oct 10am–4pm, Nov–Mar 11am–3pm, closed Dec; charge).

Below: red-brick Micklegate House.

F The Royal Gate

Every monarch from William the Conqueror onwards has passed through Micklegate Bar to enter York – except Henry VIII and Queen Victoria. Tradition has it that they asked permission to enter from the Lord Mayor. Victoria apparently visited York twice, once as princess and later as queen. Both times her visit was said to have coincided with a cholera outbreak in the city – so after the second episode she apparently remained on the royal train whenever she passed by – pulling the curtains in her carriage so she didn't have to see the offending city.

Above: royalty entered York through Micklegate Bar.

the Micklegate Run, a pub crawl from the top of the hill to the bottom. If you turn left, into Toft Green, you can visit **York Brewery** ❼ (tel: 01904 621162; www.york-brewery.co.uk; tours Mon–Sat at 12.30pm, 2pm, 3.30pm and 5pm; charge). This is a local, independent brewer which started in 1996 – the first brewery in York since the 1950s. If you join a tour you'll see how they use traditional methods to brew the beer – and then have a sample pint.

Return to Micklegate and you'll soon pass **Micklegate House** ❽. Thought to have been built for John Bourchier (1710–59), it is probably the best of the townhouses. Bourchier's ancestor, Sir John Bourchier, was one of the signatories to the execution of Charles I.

MEDIEVAL CHURCHES

Opposite Micklegate House is **Holy Trinity Church** ❾. A church has stood here for 900 years, and it is the only monastic foundation that's a place of worship to survive in York. In medieval times the pageant wagons performing the religious Mystery Plays started their tour of the city from here.

Outside the church is a replica of the stocks, which were used as a form of punishment and stood here from the 16th century until 1858. The originals are now inside the church in a glass case. Also inside is a memorial to Dr John Burton, a historian on whom Laurence Sterne is said to have modelled Dr Slop in *Tristram Shandy*. Equally of note is the Walker family memorial, honouring the parents and four brothers of Dorothy, who survived them all and erected the stone. Three of the

Above: inside Holy Trinity Church.

Above: the much-rebuilt Ouse Bridge spans the eponymous river.

brothers died in WWI – another had already died before the war started. The church has an interactive exhibition on the lives of the monks who once lived here. Off Micklegate down Trinity Lane is **Jacob's Well** ❿, a 15th-century timber-framed house with a canopied porch.

St Martin cum Gregory

The hill down Micklegate towards the river was a severe test for horse-drawn traffic, and until living memory had stone sets to give horses a better grip. **St Martin cum Gregory** ⓫, first mentioned in records in 1170, was

Below: Jacob's Well detail.

enlarged in the 14th century but is no longer used for services. It is now a centre for stained glass and events and workshops are held here (www.stainedglasscentre.org; by appointment only). Roman masonry from a Temple of Mithras nearby can be seen in the tower plinth. The medieval Butter Market used to be held outside the church, with produce being brought in from country areas for weighing and testing. William Peckitt, the glass-painter (1731–95), is buried in the chancel.

Off on the left is George Hudson Street, formerly Railway Street and before that George Hudson Street – the original name being reinstated in 1971 when the city officially forgave Hudson for the disgrace he brought on York (see box p.55). His rehabilitation continues with the council planning to commemorate his life with a monument.

St John Micklegate

St John Micklegate ⓬ is a mainly 14th- and 15th-century church, saved from decay by finding a new use in modern times – first as the Institute of Advanced Architectural Studies, then as an arts centre and now as a gastropub.

other bulky commodities came up river to this point to be unloaded by the 'common crane'. Queen's Staith was the despatch centre for the butter trade coming from the Butter Market in Micklegate.

In the 17th century some of the trade was not so savoury, as barges parked here to carry away night-soil and dung. Regulations had to be imposed to ensure that cargoes were shifted as soon as they were loaded.

ALL SAINTS CHURCH

Retrace your steps and on the upstream side of the bridge take the new elevated riverside walk by Piccolino restaurant and past the Park Inn Hotel to **All Saints, North Street** ⑬ (www. allsaints-northstreet.org.uk; Mon–Sat 10am–6pm summer, 10am–3pm winter), famous for its stained glass and 120ft (37m) spire, a striking landmark on the river frontage. Although there is Roman stonework in the structure

OVER THE OUSE

Ouse Bridge was built in 1810–21 and is the latest of at least three on the same site. The first had six arches and housed, along its entire length, public privies, a chapel, a toll booth and a prison. It appears early in the city's historical records because of a 'miraculous disaster'. So many people crowded on to it in 1154 to welcome Archbishop William into the city that it collapsed. No one died in the accident, so it was hailed as a 'miracle' and William went on to become a saint.

Another stone bridge, just as crowded with buildings including a Council Chamber, had its two central arches and the houses above carried away in a flood in 1564. The repaired bridge still had houses on it up to the early 18th century. When there was need for further repairs the city tried in vain to raise money by petitioning the House of Commons for permission to dismantle the City Walls and to use the stone and proceeds for bridge-building.

Looking downstream there is King's Staith on the left and Queen's Staith on the right – once the city's main dock area and still used by barge traffic supplemented by holiday craft. Corn and

Below: the riverfront All Saints Church.

Ⓕ Anchoress of All Saints

Dame Emma Raughton was anchoress of All Saints for many years – she was mentioned in documents dated 1421 and 1436. Anchoress comes from the Greek *anachoretes* – one who lives apart. Her home beside the church contained a couple of 'squints' – small openings that allowed her to see church services from her little cell, without joining the congregation. Rules for anchoresses of the time included one forbidding them from wearing linen next to the skin (unless made of coarse flax), another stating that their hair should be cut four times a year, and another which said the only animal they could keep (unless compelled to by need) was a cat.

and documentary references to All Saints in 1116, the main style of the church is 15th-century, when the spire was added. Softening the intrusion of the modern hotel across the road is a row of timber-framed cottages to its north side.

The wise woman of All Saints

All Saints had a live-in anchoress in the 15th century (*see box above*). She was Dame Emma Raughton, a wise woman who was said to be able to foretell the future and who received visions of the Virgin Mary – the best documented in medieval Europe. She was consulted by the kingmaker Earl of Warwick, and was said to have foretold the dual coronation of Henry VI – which took place in both France and Britain. Her prophecies were of huge political importance – no doubt why they were so well documented. She was thought to have received her visions at a large statue of the Virgin, unusually depicted without the Child;

a shrine with a recreated carving of the original statue and replica medieval flooring is the focus of present-day devotion to the Virgin. In 1910, an anchorite's cell in mock Tudor style was attached to the southwest corner of the church, with one upstairs room and an outside toilet. At least three women lived there as anchoresses, and later Brother Walter moved in – living there for some years until the early 1960s.

Superb stained glass

There was controversy in 1977 when the carvings in the church roof were restored in medieval colours, making the angels, according to some critics, look like glove puppets. The colours are now more subdued. The church windows are from the 14th and 15th centuries. The East Window of the chancel depicts John the Baptist, St Christopher and St Ann showing the Virgin how to read. Other windows illustrate the Last Days of the World, legends taken from a version of *The Prick of Conscience*, a 14th-century poem telling of the horrors and pain of the last fifteen days of the world

Below: superb All Saints stained glass.

in earthquakes and fire. Another window shows the six *Corporal Works of Mercy* as set out in St Matthew and are said to be the only complete example of this subject in stained glass in England. It shows a wealthy man visiting the sick, clothing the naked and feeding the hungry.

Among the angels in the glass in the South Choir Aisle is a medieval man wearing glasses – only two other examples of medieval spectacles appearing in stained glass are known, one in the southwest of England and the other in France. Some think that it might be a self-portrait of the glazier.

Looking across the river, there is a view of the Guildhall (see p.34).

E Eating Out

Bar Convent
17 Blossom Street; tel: 01904 643238; www.bar-convent.org.uk; Mon–Sat 8am–4pm.
Just outside the walls, the café inside this working convent serves breakfast until 11am and light lunches with a choice of salads, jacket potatoes, soups, sandwiches and cakes. It's also licensed, so you can have a beer or a glass of wine too, plus there is a lovely garden. £

Above: light and airy Bar Convent.

Brigantes Bar & Brasserie
114 Micklegate; tel: 01904 675355; www.markettowntaverns.co.uk; Mon–Fri noon–2.30pm, 6pm–9pm, Sat noon–9pm, Sun noon–8pm.
Choose from sandwiches, paninis and light lunches to chargrilled mains, washed down with an excellent pint of ale. ££

Circles Café
East Lodge, Lendal Bridge; tel: 07549 125325; Mon–Sat 10am–4.30pm, Sun 11am–4pm.
Opposite Lendal Tower, this café may be tiny but it's big on flavour and atmosphere. The lunch menu includes excellent nachos, paninis and sandwiches – try the brie, rocket and cranberry on granary. Good coffee and excellent hot chocolate. £

The Living Room
1 Bridge Street; tel: 01904 461000; www.thelivingroom.co.uk; Mon–Wed, Sun 11am–midnight, Thu–Sat 11am–1am.
Pop in this relaxed bistro for a New York-style salt beef sandwich, or some hearty Whitby cod and chips. Also on the menu: steaks, burgers and quite a few veggie options. ££

The Old Siam
126 Micklegate; tel: 01904 635162; www.theoldsiamyork.co.uk; Tue–Sat noon–2pm, 6pm–1am, Sun–Mon 6–10pm.
Located just beyond Micklegate Bar, this friendly restaurant offers visitors and locals alike an authentic Thai experience. Choose from sharing platters to start with to a huge range of curries, stir fries and set menus for mains. ££

Piccolino
18 Bridge Street; tel: 01904 521155; www.individualrestaurants.com/piccolino; Mon–Sat noon–11pm, Sun noon–10.30pm.
This smart Italian restaurant is one of a chain offering a good range of dishes. On top of pizza and pasta, they also offer mains cooked in a wood oven, such as *branzino* – seabass cooked with lemon, garlic and parsley. You'll also find charcoal-grilled chicken and steak. Desserts include tiramisu and panna cotta. ££

North York Moors National Park

Get some fresh air and discover some of Britain's loveliest countryside on a great day out

The **Moors** start north of Pickering and encompass the largest expanse of heather in England and Wales. After the agricultural order of the Vale of York they create an atmosphere of openness and freedom. The North York Moors National Park (tel: 01439 772700; www.northyorkmoors.org.uk) was designated in 1952 and covers 554 sq miles (1436 sq km), stretching from Osmotherley in the west to the Yorkshire coast in the east. Most of the land in the National Park is privately owned, and it encompasses woodland, farmland, towns and villages, as well as the Moors.

Some of Yorkshire's prettiest villages are here, like Goathland and **Farndale**, the latter famed for its springtime displays of daffodils which attracts an impressive 50,000 visitors each year. There are spectacular views too, like that from the A169 over the **Hole of Horcum**, a great amphitheatre thought to have been scooped out of the Moors at the end of the Ice Age.

WILDLIFE

The heather moorland covers a third of the land and is so vital to wildlife that it has been designated a Site of Special

the summer months and adders, Britain's only poisonous snakes, often bask in the sun; and Sutton Bank, which not only offers glorious views but also the chance to see peregrine falcons.

GETTING ACTIVE

There are excellent opportunities for walking in the National Park, which is crossed by 925 miles (1,489km) of footpaths, so you can enjoy short rambles as well as strenuous hikes.

There are many family-friendly nature trails, and some long distance ones too. The Cleveland Way runs for 110 miles (176km) from Helmsley to the coast at Filey Brigg, south of Scarborough. The famous Lyke Wake Walk (www.lyke wake.org) runs for 40 miles (64km) from Osmotherley to Ravenscar. It is often treated as a competitive walk – those completing it in 24 hours becoming members of the Lyke Wake Club.

Cyclists also have plenty of quiet country roads, forest tracks and disused railways to explore, and there is also a new Moor to Sea cycle route (www.moortoseacycle.net) which takes in some of the Park's loveliest scenery, and can easily be broken into stages. Horse riders can saddle up and explore the miles of bridleways that cover the Park – there are numerous riding centres offering treks *(see p.116)*.

Scientific Interest (SSSI). It's a great place for birdwatchers as the Moors are home to merlins (a small type of falcon), lapwings, golden plovers, meadow pipits, curlews and red grouse. Good wildlife-watching sites include Pexton Moor, northeast of Thornton le Dale, where you might see crossbills in winter and lizards in the summer; the Bridestones, striking sandstone outcrops on Grime Moor, where whinchats breed in

Above: the Cleveland Way is a picturesque long-distance trail starting from the park.
Top Left: Farndale is famed for its daffodil display. **Bottom Left**: walking in the park.
Left: red grouse on the moorland.

Steam Trains and Dinosaurs

This day-long 1½-mile (2.4km) walk starts at the National Railway Museum, crosses the river into the Museum Gardens for a picnic and takes in the striking Yorkshire Museum

York's railway heritage is immensely rich, so it's entirely fitting that the city is the location of the nation's railway museum, also the start of this tour. Allow plenty of time for your visit as it really is a fascinating place – not just for children, but for anyone interested in industrial history and the Victorian age. There are contemporary attractions too, like the Japanese bullet train.

After that the tour takes you even further back in time when you enter the Museum Gardens, which is dotted with relics from both Roman and medieval York. This is a lovely place to relax – and particularly pretty on a sunny spring day when the daffodils are in bloom. After exploring the revamped Yorkshire Museum, you'll go past reminders of York's days as the

hub of high society in the north of England: a genteel Georgian terrace and then the Theatre Royal, which helped make the city an artistic rival to London in the 18th century.

THE RAILWAY MUSEUM

The National Railway Museum ❶ (www.nrm.org.uk; daily 10am–6pm; free) is probably the biggest and best railway museum in the world. The size

Children at the NRM

There's plenty for the kids at the National Railway Museum besides the wonderful locomotives to admire. They can let off steam in the adventure playground outside and take a trip on the miniature railway (£1 per person). There's the new *Mallard Experience* ride in the Great Hall, plus a working model railway.

Above: the miniature railway.

Left: the evocative remains of St Mary's Abbey, which was once a very powerful Benedictine monastery.

of the place is impressive. The former York Motive Power Depot, it covers nearly 2 acres (0.8 hectares) and has two huge turntables. Exhibits still have direct access to the present-day railway system and occasionally go out on runs. A giant turntable inside is regularly activated. On display is a huge array of gleaming locomotives and rolling stock.

In 2013 the museum was threatened with possible closure due to government cuts. However, strength of local feeling may well save it.

Great trains

The collection covers the progression of the railways from the earliest vehicles used in mines (and run along a solid rail) and shows the extraordinary variety of experimental vehicles, wheels and gauges used. There's even a model made by Richard Trevithick, the railway pioneer.

In the Great Hall the collection's most famous locomotive, the shapely blue *Mallard (see box above)*, which broke the world speed record for steam in 1938 by reaching 126mph (203kph), takes pride of place. There's a working replica of George Stephenson's *Rocket*, which won the Rainhill

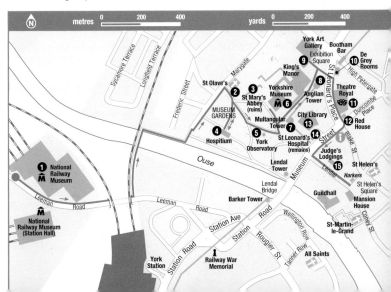

Above: impressive line-up of steam locomotives at the Railway Museum.

Trials in 1829, and his tiny *Agenoria*, from 1829, contrasts with a 190-ton steam monster, built in Britain in 1935 for China. It is so large it couldn't even operate on the British mainland. Here, too, you can see the *Evening Star*, the last steam locomotive to be built in the UK, in Swindon in 1960.

Visitors can also see – and climb aboard – a Japanese bullet train. This futuristic train is the only one on display outside Japan.

Royal connections

Also on show is a history of royalty's connection with trains and the style in which they liked to travel, including Queen Victoria's opulent saloon which

Below: Queen Victoria and Prince Albert inside the royal carriage, 1846.

was said to be her favourite travelling 'home' for the journey to Balmoral from London. Trains used by the present Royal Family, until taken out of service in 1977, are now drawn up at the platforms for everyone to see. 'Ordinary' passenger coaches range from the most primitive which ran on the Bodmin line in the 1830s to British Rail coaches from the 1950s. You can find some of these trains in the newly restored Station Hall, where you can have meal or drink alongside the stately trains.

The Warehouse and the Works

Off the Great Hall, the Warehouse displays all sorts of fascinating railway memorabilia on a rotational basis, ranging from trains to signal boxes and much more. Depending on the time of your visit, you might see an elaborate Victorian lavatory, stained-glass windows and even the bullion box from the Great Train Robbery.

The Works is a galleried area high above the museum's workshop, where visitors can watch staff hard at work renovating and repairing steam and diesel trains. You might even catch the famous *Flying Scotsman* being restored

much of its vast archives to the public. As well as giving you the chance to browse train-related books and magazines, there are also oral history recordings, railway films and an exhibition on how Britain shaped the railways of the world.

ST MARY'S ABBEY

Turn left out of the museum and take the road under the London–Scotland main railway line, before turning left again down a narrow lane and crossing the River Ouse by the footpath attached to the side of the Scarborough Railway Bridge.

Turn into Marygate and notice the medieval wall which starts at a riverside tower and runs to Marygate Tower in Bootham (see p.26). These used to be the western defences of St Mary's Abbey. On the right stands **St Olave's Church ➋**, dedicated to the patron saint of Norway and founded by the Danish Earl Siward of Northumbria sometime before 1055. The tomb of William Etty, the York artist, is in the churchyard.

– built in 1923, it was the first steam engine to reach a speed of 100mph (161kmh), which it did in 1934, and also the first to run non-stop from London to Edinburgh.

Search Engine

Railway buffs will also love Search Engine, the museum's library and research centre, which has opened up

---

⑤ Steam and Speed

The Industrial Revolution saw Britain transformed from an agricultural nation to a manufacturing powerhouse. The railways played a major role in this, allowing fast communications from places of production to ports and markets. The first steam locomotive was built by Cornishman Richard Trevithick (1771–1833). In 1801 his *Puffing Devil* transported several people along a roadway in Cornwall. Three years later another of his locomotives – this time travelling on a smooth 'rail '– carried heavy goods from an ironworks in Wales. However, the turning point came in 1825, when Northumberland engineer George Stephenson (1781–1848) drove his steam *Locomotion* on the new Stockton to Darlington railway, hauling both coal and passengers – and reaching a speed of 24mph (39kmh). The age of the train had arrived.

Above: Stephenson, the 'Father of Railways'.

Above: one of the entrances to the Museum Gardens.

Medieval might

Enter the Museum Gardens by the path alongside the church through what remains of the main gatehouse buildings of **St Mary's Abbey** ❸, founded in 1088. It is hard to imagine today, but this abbey was once one of the most powerful Benedictine monasteries in the north of England – surpassing the now more famous Fountains Abbey in both scale and importance. The abbot had immense influence and was a clergyman who commanded attention. The vast abbey covered the ground now occupied by the gardens – you can still see the walls of the nave of

Below: the York Observatory.

the abbey's church, as well as relics of the cloister – the part of the complex where the monks were allowed to speak to one another.

The abbey, as you can still see today, sat just outside York's City Walls – however it was still within the city precincts. Consequently there were frequent altercations between the abbey and the townsfolk over land rights and taxation. In the 13th century, the monks put an enormous wall around their 12 acres (5 hectares) of land in order to defend the abbey, and the defences were put to use several times. The remains of the wall are still visible – in fact it's the most complete abbey wall in the country.

The abbey survived until Henry VIII's Dissolution of the Monasteries. In the 1540s, once the monks had been removed, the abbey was turned into a palace – a handy place for the king to stay in regal splendour whenever he visited York. However, after the Dissolution, the abbey became an all too easy 'quarry' of ready-dressed stone and it started to disappear. The masonry was carted off or taken away by boat to sites all over Yorkshire, including Beverley Minster, for repair work. The mighty building became a crumbling relic. Today, all that remains of the abbey church is a romantic ruin.

The abbey's guesthouse or **Hospitium** ❹ was modernised in the 20th century, when it housed archaeological exhibits. The ground floor is medieval and is now used as a conference and wedding venue.

Stargazing

Hidden by a copse of trees is the small **York Observatory** ❺ (Thu and Sat 11.30am–2.30pm; free), which the Yorkshire Philosophical Society commissioned following the inaugural meeting of the British Association for the Advancement of Science in 1831. York had established an important role in the astronomical world in the 18th century, when two leading astronomers were based in the city. One of them, Edward Pigott, was the first Englishman to have a comet named after him.

This observatory consolidated York's reputation. It had a rotating roof, designed by John Smeaton of Eddystone Lighthouse fame, while its telescope was built in 1850 by a Thomas Cooke, who later made the largest telescope in the world. The observatory was restored and reopened in 1981. Sadly, the glare from modern city street lights now makes observations difficult.

The Museum Gardens

The **Museum Gardens** (7am–8pm summer, 7am–6pm winter) started life as botanical gardens, and are still recognised as such. Laid out in the early 19th century by the Yorkshire Philosophical Society, they boasted a large conservatory of tropical plants such as coffee, tea and cotton, as well as a water lily pond. All the trees and plants have been carefully selected and labelled – they include a monkey-puzzle tree, an ancient pear tree and an oak barked beech planted in the 1840s. This is a lovely place to have a picnic.

Ⓕ Astronomical Clock

The Observatory's Astronomical Clock dates from 1811 and tells the time according to the position of the stars. For years it was the major timepiece in York – providing the standard by which all other clocks in the city were set. It is 4mn 20s behind Greenwich Mean Time, a reminder that it was not until the 19th century that time was standardised throughout Britain.

It became a necessity with the coming of the railways, and in the 1840s railway companies started to adopt GMT as standard. It was not until 1880, however, that it became standard time right across Britain.

Below: the surviving arches along the nave of St Mary's Abbey.

Above: the Yorkshire Museum, which stands on a beautiful and tranquil 10-acre (4-hectare) botanical garden, in winter.

YORKSHIRE MUSEUM

Dominating the Gardens is the Doric-columned facade of the **Yorkshire Museum** ❻ (www.yorkshiremuseum. org.uk; daily 10am–5pm; charge, tickets valid for one year). The region's most important archaeological, geological and natural history finds are stored here – thousands of specimens of minerals, rocks and fossils, as well as the bones of prehistoric animals.

The building was the creation of William Wilkins (designer of London's National Gallery), and it was completed in 1830 for the Yorkshire Philosophical Society. This group was established in 1823 as a result of the academic excitement prompted by the discovery of prehistoric remains in the Kirkdale Cave in North Yorkshire. The Crown leased the Society the ruins of the abbey and other land in the area to build their museum. It's the second-oldest purpose-built museum in the country.

New galleries

After a £2 million refurbishment, five stunning new galleries were unveiled in 2010. The work brought the museum back to its roots, focusing on the natural sciences as well as the rich history of York. One gallery is devoted to the classical world and Roman York, displaying objects such as a striking 3rd-century statue of Mars, the Roman God of War, and a marble head of

Above: the Yorkshire Museum's prized possession – the York Helmet.

Constantine the Great, who was proclaimed emperor in the city in AD306. The gallery brings to life the realities of life in York under the Romans – including the extraordinary diversity of the peoples of the empire, who came from North Africa as well as Europe.

There is also a gallery devoted to natural history, particularly aimed at children (see box below).

The museum was partly built over the ruins of St Mary's Abbey, and relics of its ancient walls still stand within the building. These have been used to create an atmospheric gallery focusing on medieval York, highlighting the immense ecclesiastical power of the city.

Prize exhibits

Amongst the treasures on display are: the York Helmet, a fine Anglo-Saxon helmet which is one of only four ever discovered in Britain; the Ormside Bowl, a stunning piece of Anglian silversmithing decorated with fantastical beasts which was probably seized by a Viking warrior as loot and later buried with him; and the Middleham Jewel, a 15th-century diamond-shaped pendant

Above: the Gilling Sword is one of the finest Anglian weapons to be found in England.

adorned with a sapphire and engraved with religious images. It was discovered by a metal-detectorist in 1985 near Middleham in North Yorkshire. There is also the Gilling Sword, a 9th-century iron sword embellished with silver, which was found in 1976 by a nine-year-old boy while he was fishing in a Yorkshire stream. He was awarded a Blue Peter badge for his stunning find.

Ⓚ Walking with Dinosaurs

'Extinct' highlights the museum's fascinating skeletons and fossils, while telling the story of major extinctions in history. On the gallery floor you can walk – literally – in the footsteps of dinosaurs: giant footprints which were pressed into a beach and later fossilised. On the wall is the vast skeleton of Britain's largest Ichthyosaur (an astonishing 32ft/10m long), while dotted around are specimens of the victims of later extinctions – creatures like the dodo, the Great auk and the Passenger pigeon, driven over the brink by man. Children also learn about contemporary extinctions, including ones happening close to home – such as types of butterflies, bees and beetles that disappeared from Britain only in the late 20th century.

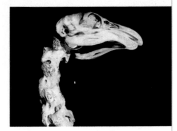

Above: skeleton on display at Extinct.

Above: King's Manor.

The History of York

The museum's auditorium presents a slick audiovisual presentation that takes you on a journey through the city's past – its buildings and its people. It's a great starting point for anyone exploring York.

The museum has also set up a 'learning' area, in the upstairs space, which has plenty of hands-on activities, workshops and exhibits. You can consult books from the extensive library,

and there are even opportunites to meet experts in the collections.

The Multangular Tower

York's best example of the 'Grandeur That Was Rome' lies outside, to the right of the Museum. The **Multangular Tower ❼** marks the southwest corner of Roman York and gives some idea of the size of the walls and towers that surrounded the Roman city about AD300. The tower is Roman up to a height of 19ft (6m), where it becomes 13th-century, having been incorporated into the city's medieval defensive wall. For a view inside, bear left of the tower to a path which leads up the embankment and through a doorway.

Turn left and walk alongside the medieval wall to the 7th- and 8th-century **Anglian Tower ❽**, the site of a tragic archaeological dig. The tower had been buried within the ramparts for centuries, but an exploratory trench cut into the earth mound in 1970 collapsed, killing the archaeologist, Jeffrey Radley. The earth mound supporting the medieval wall has been cut away to show the different heights of the city defences since Roman times.

Below: the Multangular Tower was probably built during the reign of the Emperor Septimius Severus, who was in York between 209 and 211.

Above: the remains of medieval St Leonard's Hospital.

KING'S MANOR

Return through the hole in the wall and turn right along a lane and into Exhibition Square. Turn left into the entrance of the **King's Manor ❾**. The Abbot of St Mary's used to live here until royalty took it over when the monasteries were disbanded. Henry VIII is thought to have stayed at King's Manor with Catherine Howard, James VI of Scotland visited on his way south to become James I of England, and Charles I stayed here twice when the Royal Court was in the city. His magnificent coat of arms is over the main entrance. In 1538 it then became the headquarters of the Council of the North and the residence of its Lord President. Once back in private hands it was divided into tenements, used as a girls' school, an assembly rooms for entertainments in the 18th century and then the home of the Yorkshire School for the Blind. Its present occupant is the University of York.

Turning right outside the King's Manor and across the road are the **De Grey Rooms ❿**, built in 1842 to house the officers' mess of the Yorkshire Hussars during their annual visits to York; barristers also ate their meals here during the assizes. The Rooms took their name from Earl de Grey, Colonel of the Regiment, and were used for concerts, balls and public entertainments. After WWII they were used for dances.

St Leonard's Place

The graceful sweep of tall terrace houses in **St Leonard's Place**, over to the right, was built in 1834 to provide 'genteel private residences'. To make space the Corporation tore down some 350ft (100m) of the abbey walls to the southeast of Bootham Bar. This has left the abbey's postern tower

⒡ Quaker School

St Leonard's Place runs to Exhibition Square, where it meets Bootham, the location for Bootham School. This Quaker school was founded in York in 1822 and moved to Bootham in 1846. It offered a progressive approach to education (to boys initially), with no corporal punishment and a greater focus on science and natural history than on games – it even had its own observatory. A former pupil was Joseph Rowntree, who – together with his brother – built the famous Rowntree chocolate company in York.

Above: the Bootham School bus in the 1920s.

ⓥ Picture the Minster

Duncombe Place offers a good (and accessible) viewpoint for photographers wanting to get a good shot of the Minster. About one hour before dusk, the light can often make the stonework of the ancient building look particularly picturesque. You could also walk a little further down to where it joins Museum Street and find a spot outside the Tourist Information Centre.

with a ragged wall edge stranded on the corner of the busy Bootham–Exhibition Square junction.

St Leonard's takes its name from what was the largest medieval hospital in the north of England, founded by William II. Before Henry VIII closed it down, the hospital dispensed food to the needy (including prisoners in York Castle), cared for some 400 people, mostly retired royal servants, and had a grammar school and 'bairn house' or orphanage. Charles I established a Royal Mint among its empty buildings, and in 1782 some structures were pulled down so carriages could

Below: the Theatre Royal entrance.

get better access to the new theatre. Above ground the only remains of the medieval hospital are parts of an ambulatory and chapel near the City Library. The 'genteel residences' of St Leonard's have become council offices.

THEATRE ROYAL

The history of the **Theatre Royal** ⓫ opposite started in 1744, when the first theatre was built in the cloisters of St Leonard's Hospital. It was regarded as one of the finest in the country outside London and catered for an acting company which toured local towns.

In the 18th century, manager Tate Wilkinson raised the prestige of the theatre to something approaching that of the London stage. He had to cope with unruly audiences and actors who considered his attempts at direction as an intrusion on their art. In his memoirs he records that the greatest profits came from the worst plays. The only time the 'classics' made a profit was when London stars like Sarah Siddons or John Philip Kemble came north to perform. It was Wilkinson's habit to watch new productions from the 'gods' (the seats at the top of the house) where he would hiss any bad acting. The audience was once so incensed that they threw him out of his theatre.

The theatre is still very much a thriving institution. A modern glass-fronted side extension built in 1967 provides a foyer, bars and restaurant area, as well as much-needed breathing space for theatre-goers.

DUNCOMBE PLACE

Around the corner in Duncombe Place is the imposing **Red House** ⓬, with a torch snuffer at the door. Sir William Robinson, a Lord Mayor, built the house for himself, but in 1724 was pressured by the city to turn it into the official home for all the city's Lord Mayors. Sir William refused, so the city built the

Above: the picture-perfect Red House.

Mansion House instead *(see p.33)*. The Red House is now an antiques centre.

Turning one's back on York Minster, go down Museum Street towards the river passing the **City Library** ⑬ on the right. The first public library in York, it was established by Joseph Rowntree and moved here in 1927. He had previously started a library for his factory workers in 1885 – a typical philanthropic gesture from this social reformer (although he did make workers pay a penny a week to help keep it open). By the library are the only above-ground remains of **St Leonard's Hospital** ⑭. At the entrance to the Museum Gardens turn left into Lendal.

The **Judges Lodgings** ⑮ (set back from the road) are where, from 1802, the Assize judges stayed having arrived with much pomp in the city to demand the sheriff to deliver up for judgement everyone held in the city jails. The building is now a hotel and restaurant.

Continue along Lendal to St Helen's Square, where this tour ends, on the site of the Praetorian Gate, the main entrance to Roman York.

▣ Eating Out

Harkers
1 St Helen's Square; tel: 01904 672795; 10am–10pm.
Situated in a grand building that formerly belonged to the Yorkshire Insurance Company, Harkers occupies a prime position in central York. It's a bar-restaurant, so you can come just for a drink or for something to eat. Dishes on offer include steak sandwiches, salmon or chicken salad, sharing platters, cod and chips and Gloucester Old Spot sausages. On fine days there are a few seats outside on the square. ££

Judges Lodgings
9 Lendal; tel: 01904 638733; www.judgeslodgings.com; daily 11am–9pm.
Lots of old British favourites on the menu at this relaxed hotel eatery: local sausages of the day, steak and ale pie, as well as hearty sandwiches. There are also some real ales available. Eat outside in the spacious courtyard, or inside in the cosy cellar bar. ££

Tour 6

Narrow Streets and Hidden Treasures

Starting with a chocolate tour, this 2-mile (3.2km) half-day tour circles the narrow streets in the city centre taking in a fine church, a picturesque pub and a couple of museums

One of the joys of walking around York is in exploring its maze of atmospheric, narrow streets. The names, too, are fascinating, providing a constant reminder of the city's rich heritage. This walk is full of such reminders – particularly as it takes you along the street with the most memorable (and tongue-twisting) name of all: Whip-ma-whop-ma-gate. You'll also stroll down lively Goodramgate, off which is hidden one of the city's finest churches.

In contrast to the huddled buildings on the streets, you get a sense of space when you climb the walls and stroll above the city, where you're rewarded with fine views of the Minster.

Highlights

- York's Chocolate Story
- Goodramgate
- Holy Trinity
- Whip-Ma-Whop-Ma-Gate
- DIG
- Black Swan Public House
- Bar Walls

YORK'S CHOCOLATE STORY

In **King's Square,** where you'll find street performers entertaining the crowds (see p.42), is **York's Chocolate Story ❶** (King's Square, tel: 0845

Left: shops and cafés line up on popular Low Petergate.

498 9411; www.yorkschocolatestory.com; daily 10am–6pm; charge); which opened in 2012. This is not a museum, but an interactive experience into the world of chocolate and its importance to the city. It is particularly appealing to families and, of course, chocoholics of all ages, and there are plenty of chances to taste. The tour begins in the Story Zone where you will learn about the origins of chocolate, followed by the impact of the Quaker families, in particular Rowntree and Terry, on employment in York. In the Factory Zone the emphasis is on production, ethical commitments and the role of the chocolatier. Finally the Indulgence Zone is where you part with your money at the café and shop. There are also regular demonstrations and events. To learn more about chocolate manufacture in York, check out the Chocolate Trail (see p.11).

LOW PETERGATE

Head up **Low Petergate** towards the Minster's twin towers, which can be

seen above the distant rooftops. This is an attractive narrow street of shops (see box below) with their overhanging upper storeys dating from Tudor and early Stuart times. Just beneath the road surface lies the wide, stone-flagged Via Principia of Roman York.

On the right is the even narrower **Hornpot Lane**, so called since the 13th century. An archaeological dig in 1957–8 found the reason: a pit was discovered containing waste materials which showed that the local industry had been making items out of horn. The lane leads to Holy Trinity Church, which you'll see later on this tour.

S Low Petergate Shops

For ladies' clothes there's Reiss, Noa Noa and Giselle, as well as Sarah Coggles and Miss Diva for the young. Molly Brown's sells covetable little dresses and accessories. Bookworms can browse at the Oxfam bookshop, and foodies can taste various flavoured oils at Vom Fass. In nearby Goodramgate, modern art-lovers will enjoy tiny gallery Artestee.

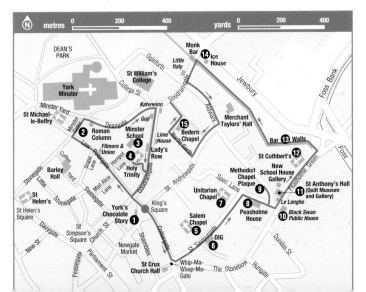

To the left is, somewhat politically incorrectly, **Mad Alice Lane**, one of York's many narrow snickleways. The lane is named after Alice Smith, who was hanged in the 1830s and was reputedly insane. On the right you'll see the Georgian frontage of what was York College for Girls; founded in 1907, it closed in 1997 and is now an Italian restaurant.

Minster Gates

At **Minster Gates** ❷ turn right to face the cathedral's south door. In the 13th century the Minster was surrounded by a 12ft (3.5m) wall, and this was one of the four entrances. Few traces of the wall remain. This section was demolished along with houses in Petergate when Duncombe Place was built in the 19th century. Opposite the Minster you'll notice a large Roman column. Found in 1969 during an excavation, it's a striking reminder of the city's previous role as a major outpost of empire. A plaque on the column says that it stood in the great hall of the 6th legion in the 4th century.

Deangate

Through Minster Gates, turn right into Deangate. In 1903 it seemed a good idea to demolish property close to the cathedral and create a new road, but the Minster authorities came to regret it. Deangate became a major thoroughfare with heavy lorries shaking the cathedral's foundations. It was not until 1990 that the Minster authorities persuaded the City Council to stop the traffic and pedestrianise the area.

Tucked away on the right behind a small playing field is the **Minster School** ❸, which was revived from ancient times in 1903 and installed in the building. Most of the children educated here are choristers in the cathedral. Before traffic was banned the students daily doffed their caps to

Above: cricket practice in the grounds of Minster School.

waiting motorists as they processed over the pedestrian crossing into the cathedral for services. Next door is the **Minster Stoneyard**. If the gates are open, giant overhead saws can be seen cutting through blocks of stone as part of the continual repair work on the cathedral.

GOODRAMGATE

Turn right into Goodramgate, where antique shops and boutiques occupy still more Tudor houses with half-

🎦 Spot the Face

Young children in Holy Trinity Church should enjoy looking out for the little face carved on the first column as you come through the door (you'll need to lift them up to see it). It looks like a man scratching his chin. To the left of the altar, in the North Aisle, is a 13th-century grave cover depicting a fish and a cooking pot. This is taken to be a sign that the person originally interred beneath it was a fishmonger.

timbered upper storeys. On the right is **Lady's Row**, a line of 11 tenements which have retained elements of their 14th-century origins. They date back to 1316 and are considered by many to be the oldest row of houses in Britain. Opposite them is a 20th-century development of pillarless concrete arches over shop fronts. It caused such an outcry in the 1960s that a strict watch was kept on all city-centre 'improvements' thereafter. Ironically, it is now protected as a prime example of 1960s architecture.

Holy Trinity Church

An iron gateway on the right gives entry to one of the prettiest, most secluded yet almost forgotten churches in York, **Holy Trinity, Goodramgate** ❹ (Tue–Sat 10am–4pm, Sun–Mon noon–4pm). Stepping out of the busy street into a quiet churchyard, one is faced with a venerable building with Jacobean box pews, uneven floors and an all-pervading atmosphere of antiquity.

The church was built in 1250–1500, but was rearranged after the Reformation in a style often referred to as a 'Prayer Book' interior. The altar was no longer the focus of attention; instead the congregation was to focus

Above: secluded, medieval Holy Trinity, Goodramgate.

on the preaching – hence why some of the pews have their backs to the altar. The church has a two-tier pulpit (1785) and a reredos with the Ten Commandments, Creed and Lord's Prayer written out for worshippers. One can read the undulating floor for a history of York notables – in front of the communion rails is the stone marking the resting place of Charles II's valet. The Side Chapel has a 'squint' (a hole in the wall – sometimes called a hagioscope), so the priest at the chapel altar (where the

Below: the street with a tongue-twister of a name, Whip-Ma-Whop-Ma-Gate.

WHIP·MA·WHOP·MA·GATE

Ⓚ DIG Deep

At DIG, budding young archaeologists explore recreated excavation pits (filled with clean fake soil) which contain some real 'finds', picking through trays of 'dig debris' and sorting out bones, teeth and bits of pottery. High-tech films and hologram 'guides' give information on digging techniques. You also look through microscopes to view slides of fossilised insects such as fleas and cockroaches and get a close-up look at a mock grave containing a skeleton.

Above: comparing dig 'finds'.

wealthy would once have worshipped separately) could see the high altar, in order to coordinate the service.

Holy Trinity's interior was saved from alteration due to the congregation dwindling in the 1800s, so the authorities did not consider it worth spending money on. In 1972 it was officially declared redundant, but three services are held a year (the one at Advent is candlelit, as the church has

Below: DIG is another success story from York's Archaeological Trust.

no electricity). The 15th-century tower has an unusual saddleback roof and same-era glass in the East Window. Hornpot Lane, already seen from Petergate, leads into a corner of the churchyard.

WHIP-MA-WHOP-MA-GATE

Keep right and back into King's Square and down Colliergate, which becomes the shortest street in York (only some 35yds/m long), but the one with the longest name: **Whip-Ma-Whop-Ma-Gate**. Some think this is a corruption of 'whitnourwhatnourgate' (neither one thing nor the other) or an ironic Viking term for 'What a Street' (a reference to how short it is). Others consider the name came about because, in later years, it was close to the site of the public whipping post in Pavement. In medieval times the city also had an annual Whip Dog Day. A priest celebrating the mass once dropped a wafer and a dog ran off with it, so every St Luke's Day the custom was for schoolboys to remember the incident by whipping all dogs in the streets. It is said that a man could also whip his wife here if she was drunk in public – some claim that this has never been repealed.

Above: the cosy, oak-panelled interior of the Black Swan Public House.

Down St Saviourgate on the left is the **Salem Chapel ❺**, with an Ionic portico and its entrance approached by a flight of steps. In its 19th-century heyday it could fit nearly 1,700 people.

DIG

The inside of the redundant church of St Saviour opposite has been cleverly adapted to become **DIG ❻** (tel: 01904 615505; www.digyork. co.uk; daily 10am–5pm, last entry 4pm; charge, pre-booking suggested for tours at busy times) – another offshoot of the enterprising York Archaeological Trust which created the Jorvik Viking Centre *(see p.44)*. Here, a guided tour introduces visitors to the archaeological arts *(see box above)*.

Further down St Saviourgate there are Georgian townhouses to the right and on the left the **Unitarian Chapel ❼**, the earliest of York's surviving Nonconformist churches (1692–3). Charles Wellbeloved, the eminent scholar and historian, was a minister here until 1858 and is buried here.

PEASHOLME

At the end of St Saviourgate turn right past **Peasholme House ❽**, a fine Georgian building from 1752 which was restored by the York Civic Trust in 1975 and turned into offices. If you then briefly turn left into Aldwark, and stroll partway up, you'll see a plaque

on the wall on the left-hand side commemorating the use of this stark, plain building as the city's first **Methodist chapel ❾**. John Wesley preached at the opening service in 1759 and returned many times. Its religious use was discontinued in 1805 when larger premises were needed.

THE BLACK SWAN

Across the busy Peasholme Green is the 13th-century **Black Swan Public House ❿**, black and white timber-framed on the outside and with oak-panelled rooms and open fires within *(see Eating Out, p.85)*. Sir Martin Bowes, treasurer of the Royal Mint in Elizabeth I's time and Lord Mayor of London, had his family home here. Born in the house was the mother of General Wolfe who died in the assault on Quebec in 1759. The Black Swan was also a famous coaching inn, and illegal cockfighting took place on the first floor. A grill overlooks the stairs, so someone could warn against the approach of the law.

The commercial buildings to the right of the pub cover what used to

Below: Peasholme House.

be the notorious Hungate slums. They were cleared before WWII and a new road, Stonebow, laid out. The name came from an ancient lane which could be a clue to York's greatest mystery: where is the Roman amphitheatre? The Viking-derived name 'stonebow' could be a reference to amphitheatre ruins which the invaders may have found still standing when they took over the city.

ST ANTHONY'S HALL

Turn left into Peasholme Green to **St Anthony's Hall** ⓫. The 15th-century guildhall of St Anthony was until recently in the care of York University and housed diocesan records as part of the Borthwick Institute of Historical Research. The outside of the building is a mixture of stone and brick, while the main hall has a timbered ceiling with a number of fine carved rib joints or bosses.

After the Dissolution of the Monasteries the Corporation took over the guild and found a variety of uses for their new acquisition. It has been a workhouse, a prison, a knitting school for poor children, a military hospital during the Civil War and, in the early 18th century, the home of the Blue Coat School. It is now home to the **Quilt Museum and Gallery** (tel: 01904 613242; www.quilt museum.org.uk; Feb–Nov Mon–Sat 10am–4pm; charge). The Bailey Gallery, where boys from the Blue Coat School used to dine, is now used as an exhibition space to display both historic and contemporary textiles. There is also a programme of 'hands-on' events, activities and workshops for those interested in the crafts of quilting and patchwork.

Creative corner

Hidden away in the courtyard, by the museum, is the **New School House Gallery** (tel: 01904 653603, www.schoolhousegallery.co.uk, Tue–Sat 10am–5pm), a contemporary art gallery with a changing programme of exhibitions, from photographs to porcelain, installations to origami. The gallery shop also stocks items such as hand-carved bowls, contemporary textiles and sleek ceramics.

Next door, **St Cuthbert's Church** ⓬ has an unusual success story. On the brink of being declared surplus to requirements in the 1970s, its congregation suddenly blossomed and outgrew the 16th-century church and worshippers had to move into the much larger St Michael-le-Belfry near the Minster. A free-standing glass 'bubble' was built inside St Cuthbert's to create offices and rooms for the St Michael's administration centre. The design won a prestigious architectural award in 1984.

JEWBURY AND THE WALLS

Continue past St Cuthbert's and at the busy road junction over the River Foss climb up the steps onto the **Bar**

Ⓖ Secret Garden

The entrance to the Quilt Museum is reached through a gate in the wall, which hides a lovely garden. This is contemporary in style, with paved areas, arches, sculptural features and beds of fragrant plants. It's a great spot to sit and relax, read a book or even have a quiet picnic lunch.

Above: the paved secret garden.

Above: after many uses, St Anthony's Hall now houses the Quilt Museum.

Walls ⓭. A plaque explains that there was always a break in the walls here (between Layerthorpe Bridge and the Red Tower), because of the presence of a huge lake known as the King's Fishpool. It was so large that it functioned as a defence, so there was no need for a wall; the lake has long gone. The multi-storey car park seen from the walls covers the site of **Jewbury**, an area acquired by York's Jewish community in Henry II's reign which they later used as a cemetery. Many of the city's Jews were forced to commit suicide at Clifford's Tower in 1190, while a mob waited for them outside. There is a commemorative plaque in English and Hebrew. In the 19th century, a hoard of coins and a medieval Jewish amulet were found.

As you walk along the wall, you can look down and see **Aldwark** (meaning old fortifications), an area of neat new courtyards and townhouses built since 1968 as part of a plan to bring people back to live in the city centre. It has been a residential success story. You also get an aerial view of the remains of some of the Roman walls, which formed part of the Eboracum fortress, and a fine view of the Minster. As you approach Monk Bar, look

down on a brick 'igloo' or **Ice House ⓮** outside the walls. This structure was erected in 1800 to store ice for keeping larders cool. The ice was straw-packed in a deep pit and the brick dome covered with soil.

The 14th-century Monk Bar is four storeys high. It has a working portcullis and once functioned as a self-contained fortress, with 'murder-holes' – slits in the stonework which made it easy to fire arrows or drop missiles on attackers (see also p.24).

Above: Monk Bar.

Above: make sure to have some Yorkshire parkin during your stay.

MERCHANT TAYLORS' HALL

Leaving the walls at Monk Bar, walk into the city and turn left into Aldwark to the **Merchant Taylors' Hall** (not open to the public). Built in 1415, the building was for a long time in the hands of the Confraternity of St John, before being taken over by another powerful York guild formed in 1662 by the amalgamation of three groups of medieval craftsmen – the tailors, drapers and hosiers. It is the only example of a craft guildhall in the city and has a 60ft (18m) long Great Hall, with a 14th-century arch braced roof. Guild members controlled the city's clothing trade but lost power when guild monopolies were removed in the early 19th century. The hall has since been used for a variety of social functions.

The Aldwark area, once filled with derelict warehouses, has been dramatically revived with townhouses. The restoration and conversion into residential accommodation of the Georgian-fronted **Oliver Sheldon House** next door to the hall was part of the 'bring back the people' plan (see p.83). The house is named after the founder and secretary of the York Civic Trust who died in 1951.

Bedern Chapel

Turn right into St Andrewgate and right again into Bedern. On the left, **Bedern Chapel** ⓰ was consecrated in 1349 as the chapel for the Vicars Choral of the Minster. *Bedern* is Anglo-Saxon for house of prayer. The chapel is now the workshop for glaziers restoring the precious windows of the Minster. The archway ahead leads into Goodramgate and back to the city centre.

⒡ Art of Glass

Get a behind-the-scenes glimpse of stained-glass conservation with a tour of Bedern Chapel. A specialist guide will take you round, as conservators work on the glass, and explain the techniques and skills required. The tours take place on Mondays, Wednesdays and Fridays at 2pm, and leave from the Undercroft Desk in the Minster. Tours must be pre-booked (tel: 0844 939 0011; www.yorkglaziertrust.org; charge).

Above: restored Minster work.

ⓔ Eating Out

Black Swan
Peasholme Green; tel: 01904 679131; www.blackswanyork.com; food served Mon–Fri noon–2.45pm and 5–7.45pm, Sat–Sun noon–4.45pm.
This picturesque pub dished up hearty traditional meals; look out for pigeon pie with roast potatoes, steak and ale pie, or rabbit stew. Giant Yorkshire puddings with roast beef and onion gravy are also very popular. There are a few options for vegetarians, as well as a special children's menu. ££

Filmore & Union
62a Low Petergate; tel: 01904 654123; www.filmoreandunion.co.uk; Mon–Sat 8am–10pm, Sun 9am–9.30pm.
A street level deli/café and a stylish first-floor restaurant with open kitchen comprise this venue that offers great seasonal food for breakfast, lunch and dinner. The daily changing menu features light snacks including bagels, salads and soups, with evening mains such as baked Asian spiced mullet. Fresh and healthy are the key words here. ££

Goji
36 Goodramgate; tel: 01904 622614; www.gojicafe.co.uk; Sun–Thu 11am–4.30pm, Fri 11am–4.30pm, 6.30–11pm, Sat 9.30am–5pm and 6.30–11pm.
This vegetarian and vegan café-deli offers a wide range of vegetarian snacks and light meals, with everything from hummous with pitta bread to mushroom burgers. There's a courtyard area for eating out on sunny days. Goji also opens some evenings, when it serves tasty meals such as porcini mushroom and crushed walnut risotto to start, followed by open buckwheat crêpe topped with roasted vegetables. Desserts range from organic ice creams to apple and calvados puff pastry tart. ££

Kafeneion
39 Goodramgate; tel: 01904 655068; www.kafeneion.co.uk; Mon–Wed, Sun 9am–5.30pm, Thu–Sat 9am–late.
Don't be put off by the small and rather unassuming exterior as this café has some of the best coffee in town. Scrumptious cakes, sandwiches and paninis on offer. You can get tasty meze, platters and cocktails three evenings a week. Courtyard seating. ££

Le Langhe
The Old Coach House, Peasholme Green; tel: 01904 622584; www.lelanghe.co.uk; café: Mon–Thu 10.30am–5.30pm, Fri 10am–5.30pm, Sat 9.30am–5.30pm; restaurant: Fri–Sat 7pm–finish.
Food and wine imported from Italy are on the menu at this attractive little deli-restaurant which backs onto the garden by the Quilt Museum. The menu changes frequently, depending on the best produce available. You can come during the day for salads, a cheese board or pasta dishes. In the evenings, you could try the special seven-course tasting menu. ££

Lime House Restaurant
55 Goodramgate; tel: 01904 632734; www.limehouserestaurant-york.co.uk; Tue–Sat noon–2pm, 6.30–9.30pm.
With fine Yorkshire produce on the menu, this restaurant offers imaginative modern British cuisine. Choose rump of venison rolled in herbs, smoked rack of Yorkshire lamb or pan-fried fillet of Yorkshire beef. Vegetarians might have a butternut squash risotto or a savoury bread pudding with cheese, mushrooms and leeks. Good-value set meals. ££

Little Italy
12 Goodramgate; tel: 01904 623539; www.littleitalyrestaurantyork.co.uk; Mon–Tue, Thu 5pm–10pm, Fri 11.30am–2.30pm, 5–10pm, Sat 11.30am–3pm, 5–10pm, Sun 11.30am–3pm, 4.30–9pm.
This traditional Italian restaurant is a relaxed place to have pasta dishes, grills and meaty main courses such as fillet steak flambéed with port, finished with truffle cream and peppercorn sauce, or prawns in garlic and white wine. There are some fish dishes too. ££

From Riches to Rags

This 2-mile (3km) tour starts in the richest area of medieval York and visits a notorious highwayman's grave en route; you can take an optional stroll along the walls or the riverside

This walk takes you from the bustling heart of York to parts of the city that aren't on the main tourist trail. Medieval splendour is in evidence at the Merchant Adventurers' Hall – a reminder that trade has always played a major role in the life of the city. You then enter an area once considered an appalling slum, but which has since been regenerated. After taking in Walmgate Bar, you walk to Dick Turpin's Grave, just inside the city walls. If you feel like it, you can then extend the tour by walking along the walls, or following a path that runs beside the river.

FOSSGATE

Leave **Pavement** by a narrow lane alongside **Herbert House** *(see p.44)* and into **Lady Peckitt's Yard** ❶ for

Highlights

- Lady Peckitt's Yard
- Fossgate
- Merchant Adventurers' Hall
- Walmgate Bar
- Dick Turpin's Grave

a fascinating glimpse of how the city must have looked in Tudor times. Black and white half-timbered buildings crowd together and at one point make a bridge over the lane. The lane was originally called Bake House Lane, but later named after the wife of John Peckitt, who was Lord Mayor in 1702. It is a reference to a local saying that 'the mayor was a Lord for a year and a day, his wife is a Lady for ever and aye'. Lady Peckitt is said to haunt the nearby Golden Fleece pub, which claims to be the most haunted premises in York.

The lane emerges in Fossgate, where the richest of the city's medieval merchants used to live. The furniture store opposite, just to the right, however, is far from medieval. It has a startling terracotta tiled half-domed entrance decorated with swags of fruits in the Venetian style. It dates from 1911, when the premises were converted into the **Electric Cinema ❷**. Fossgate has taken on a new lease of life as a 21st-century foodie haven, with a generous clutch of good restaurants lining the pavements.

Merchant Adventurers' Hall
Further down Fossgate on the right is a stone-framed doorway under the coat of arms of the York Merchant

Left: the tranquil setting of Fossbridge over the River Foss. **Above**: entrance to Lady Peckitt's Yard.

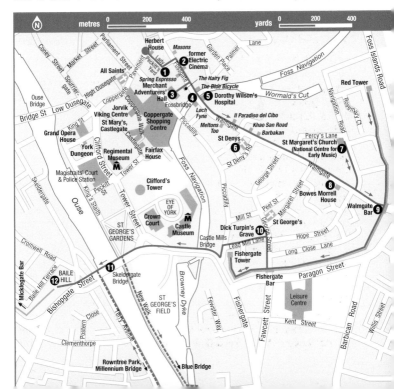

Above: the lovely Merchant Adventurers' Hall is a popular wedding venue.

Adventurers – two winged horses supporting a shield and the motto: *Dieu Nous Donne Bonne Adventure*. The door leads to the stunning **Merchant Adventurers' Hall ❸** (tel: 01904 654818; www.theyorkcompany.co.uk; Mar–Oct Mon–Thu 9am–5pm, Fri–Sat 9am–3.30pm, Sun 11am–4pm, Nov–Feb Mon–Thu 10am–4pm, Fri–Sat 10am–3.30pm; charge).

This is the largest timber-framed building in the city and the home of the most powerful of the York guilds, which closely guarded its trade with the outside world. The Great Hall has a massive timber-framed roof supported on braced beams and with Elizabethan panelling and uneven planked floor. Banners and portraits of past masters invoke the hall's heyday – illustrious figures such as George Hudson, George Leeman, Sir Joseph Terry and Joseph Rowntree were all members.

In smaller rooms you will find fine furniture and clocks – most notable is the 'evidence chest' in the governor's parlour, which dates back to the 1340s and is older than the Hall itself. This rather battered-looking oak chest would have held important documents like the company accounts.

The 14th-century stone undercroft is used for receptions and contains the Trinity Chapel with late-17th century seating and pulpit. Although starting life as a religious institution in 1357, the Guild soon went into business and played a leading role in the city's medieval prosperity. The Guild still holds

Above: the Guild's banners still hang inside the Hall.

meetings in its hall when its members wear robes and an 18th-century mace is carried before the Master. On leaving the hall, detour around to the grassed area in front for a better view of the half-timbered exterior.

Fossbridge

Back in Fossgate, walk down to the arched and balustraded **Fossbridge** ❹, built in 1811. The previous bridge was crowded with houses. Tenants were forbidden to put windows on the river side of their properties because they were used to dump rubbish into the river.

Over the bridge on the left, stone inscriptions high on the house wall (rather hard to read now) recall that this was **Dorothy Wilson's Hospital** ❺, which the good lady endowed in 1717 for the maintenance of 10 poor women and to teach 20 poor boys reading and writing. A monument in St Denys Church up the road recounts her other charitable work.

WALMGATE

Enter **Walmgate**, an area which is coming back to life after a grim and sordid past. Nineteenth-century records tell of a largely immigrant Irish population living here in wretched conditions,

the women sitting on the kerb stones and smoking their pipes. As late as 1901 a 500yd/m long stretch of road to Walmgate Bar boasted 20 public houses. Slum clearances have left gaps, and the old properties that do survive look isolated among the new shops and businesses that are moving back.

St Denys Church ❻ on the right was first recorded c.1154, although there was a church on this site in Saxon times. It has windows of exceptionally fine medieval glass – some of which is the oldest in York. At one time St Denys had a soaring 116ft spire, but this was damaged in 1644 during the Civil War and later destroyed completely by lightning. A vault belonging to the Percy family is thought to lie beneath the South Aisle. One of the family, Henry, Earl of Northumberland, who was killed at the Battle of Towton in 1461, is believed to be buried here.

Early Music Centre

St Margaret's Church ❼, largely rebuilt in 1851, has lost its medieval setting completely and is set back among trees with a backdrop of warehouses and council flats. Vestiges of the 17th-century building remain in the tracery of some windows but the doorway of the porch is 12th-century Romanesque

Above: Yorkshire belle.

and thought to have come from St Nicholas's Church in Lawrence Street. It is richly carved with the signs of the zodiac, the Labours of the Months and with stories from Aesop's fables. It is hard to make out the detail of the carvings today, but you should be able to spot some mythical creatures playing musical instruments. The restored church is now the National Centre for Early Music (www.ncem.co.uk; box office: 01904 658338), which runs the annual Early Music Festival *(see p.41)*, as well as concerts and activities.

Also isolated by modernity across the street is **Bowes Morrell House ❽**, a 14th-century timber-framed structure restored and put into commercial use by the York Civic Trust in 1966.

Walmgate Bar

Walmgate ends at the 12th-century **Walmgate Bar ❾**, the most complete of the city's gateways. It's the only one with its barbican intact; the portcullis hangs in its slot above the roadway and the 15th-century inner wooden door has its wicket gate still in place. At one time the heads of traitors would have been displayed on the building. The bar was badly battered by Parliamentarian cannon fire during the Civil War siege of the city in 1644 and had to be extensively repaired. On the inner face of the gateway is an Elizabethan addition – a wood and

❺ The Civil War

York was an important city in the reign of Charles I. He set up a Royal Mint here and as conflict between him and Parliament increased, he established a printing press to circulate royal propaganda. When the Civil War (1641–51) broke out, York became a Royalist stronghold. In 1644 the city was surrounded and besieged by Parliamentarians, who eventually breached the defences. Shortly afterwards the Royalist forces were decisively beaten at the battle of Marston Moor, a few miles outside the city. York surrendered and the Parliamentarian Sir Thomas Fairfax was named governor of the city. Luckily he ordered that buildings were not to be ransacked – thus saving the Minster and other city churches from destruction.

Above: Charles I visited York a couple of times, staying at King's Manor.

Above: Walmgate Bar was the subject of some of the fiercest attacks by Parliamentarians during the siege of York in 1644.

plaster building with an ornamental palisade. Walmgate Bar was leased out as a home from at least the 14th century up until the 1950s.

THE RED TOWER

If you were to walk onto the wall and to your left now, you'd find that the wall walk comes to a dead end after nearly a quarter of a mile at the **Red Tower**. This was first referred to in the early 16th century as the 'rede' tower, and was unusual in that it wasn't built of stone, but of brick, which was much cheaper. This didn't go down well with the city's stonemasons, and led to several bursts of unrest.

The land between the tower and the restart of the wall at Peasholme Green was marshy and regarded as militarily impassable, so there was no need to extend the wall over the land here. William the Conqueror dammed the River Foss to get water into his castle ditches and the flooded area became a valuable royal fishpond – the King's Fishpool.

DICK TURPIN'S GRAVE

This tour goes onto the walls but turns to the right from Walmgate Bar.

The parapet walk here runs for just over a quarter of a mile to Fishergate Bar, passing on the way the city's **York Barbican** and swimming pool, built on the city's former cattle market. The centre, reopened in 2011, is now home to a 1,400-seat multipurpose entertainment venue.

Descend at Fishergate Bar. You can climb up to the walls again and proceed a short distance to a dead end at Fishergate Tower. Built between 1502 and 1507, the tower, in a somewhat neglected state, is being restored with the aim to open it up as an exhibition space and café. Back at the Bar turn right into George Street and in St George's Burial Ground, across the road from the actual church, is **Dick Turpin's Grave ⑩**. A modern tombstone replaces the original worn-away stone. The tombstone bears his real name, as well as the alias John Palmer he was using when he was arrested – Palmer was his mother's maiden name. After being hanged for highway robbery in 1735, Turpin was buried here twice. The first time the corpse was stolen but was subsequently retrieved by a mob and reburied.

Above: Skeldergate Bridge was built as a toll bridge; a small arch by the former tollhouse at the east end of the bridge was designed to open up for tall ships.

RAMPARTS AND RIVERS

Back towards the Bar, head down Lead Mill Lane on the right and cross the Foss at Castle Mills Bridge. To the left beyond the locks are the modern flood barriers controlling the flow of the Foss into the Ouse. Cross the Ouse via **Skeldergate Bridge ⑪** and complete the circuit of the city walls. Until 1875, when the bridge was built, a ferry took people across the river at this point. Downstream on the nearside bank is St George's Field where hangings took place. The spectre of Dick Turpin is said to haunt the site – he wears a black cape and gallops across it on his horse.

The Bar Walls start again after the bridge at **Baile Hill ⑫**, a large mound once topped by another of William the Conqueror's wooden and moated castles. The hill was planted with trees in the early 18th century; a century later a prison was built here, only to be demolished in 1880 and the stone used for the foundations of the nearby bridge.

A pleasant optional half-mile walk along the ramparts with distant views of the Minster over the chimney pots ends at **Micklegate Bar** (see p.56).

NEW WALK

Another option would be not to cross Skeldergate Bridge, but instead to turn left and stroll along New Walk. This tree-lined avenue was created in the early 18th century, and was intended as a genteel riverside promenade for the fashionable Georgian classes flocking to York at that time. You pass St George's Field, cross a small bridge (Blue Bridge) and then continue down to cross the river at the new Millennium Bridge.

At this point you turn back towards the city and walk back along the other side of the river, passing Rowntree Park, which was gifted to the city in 1921 by the Rowntree chocolate company as a memorial to their staff who served and died in WWI. The walk is about 2 miles (3km) and perfect on a summer's day for a picnic.

Ⓕ Haunted City

York is often referred to as the most haunted city in Britain, with reports of around 500 different ghostly happenings. Hauntings include a young girl often seen watching funerals at All Saints, Pavement, the legs of a man seen descending the stairs at the Black Swan pub, and a Roman soldier who tramps around the Dean Court Hotel. People walking under Bedern Arch have reported the sound of children giggling, and have said that they've felt a small child take their hand, while Sir Thomas Percy supposedly haunts Holy Trinity churchyard on Goodramgate, looking for his severed head. There are plenty of ghost walks and trails to choose from, leaving every night (see p.123).

E Eating Out

Barbakan
58 Walmgate; tel: 01904 672474;
www.deli-barbakan.co.uk; Mon
10am–3pm, Tue–Sat 10am–3pm,
6–10pm, Sun noon–9pm.
With rave reviews, Barbakan brings
a taste of Poland to York. Great for
a coffee or light lunch from the café
menu or try something more substantial from the restaurant menu. Expect
the likes of rolled stuffed pancakes
with mushrooms or meat, followed by
Polish hunter's stew or pork loin filled
with ham and cheese. ££

The Blue Bicycle
34 Fossgate; tel: 01904 673990;
www.thebluebicycle.com; Mon–Wed
6–9.30pm, Thu–Sun noon–2.30pm,
6–9.30pm (Sun until 9pm).
This atmospheric restaurant focuses
on modern British food with a foreign
twist. Dishes include baked loin of
spiced monkfish, crayfish with peas
and wild rice, twice-baked Provençal
herb soufflé or chargrilled fillet of
Yorkshire beef with fondant potato.
For dessert, choose from caramelised
apple cheesecake and deconstructed
lemon meringue pie. £££

Il Paradiso del Cibo
40 Walmgate; 01904 611444; www.
ilparadisodelcibo.com; Mon–Sat
12.30–3pm, 6–10pm (Sun summer
only).
Cosy Italian restaurant with all pasta
dishes made with the finest Italian
ingredients and free range eggs.
Traditional pizzas come with a range
of homemade toppings and there is
plenty of choice for vegetarians, too.
££

Khao San Road
50–52 Walmgate; tel: 01904 635999;
Tue–Thu 5pm–10pm, Fri–Sat noon–
10pm, Sun noon–9pm.
A popular Thai restaurant, which can
get busy, but the service is quick.
Good range of dishes from traditional
Thai curries to those straight from the
wok. Starters include steamed mussels,
served with a variety of sauces. ££

Loch Fyne
12 Walmgate; tel: 01904 650910;
www.lochfynerestaurants.com; Mon–
Thu 11.30am–10pm, Sat 9am–11pm,
Sun 9am–10pm.
This chain of seafood restaurants
serves fresh Scottish produce such as
Loch Fyne oysters, smoked salmon,
kippers and mussels. The focus is on
sustainably produced fish – so you'll
find farmed gilt head bream and
line-caught haddock. There are a few
meat dishes as well as a vegetarian
pasta option. £££

Masons
13 Fossgate; tel: 01904 611919;
www.masonsbarbistro.co.uk; Mon–Fri
noon–3pm, 5.30–9pm (Fri until 9.30),
Sat noon–9.30pm, Sun noon–7.30pm.
Situated in a former grocer's shop,
this pleasant wine bar-restaurant has
scrubbed wooden tables and a menu
featuring a variety of burgers, including a delicious veggie one. Plus sharing platters, kebabs, grills and classic
dishes. ££

Meltons Too
25 Walmgate; tel: 01904 629222;
www.meltonstoo.co.uk; Mon–Sat
10.30am–midnight, Sun until 11pm.
Oak beams and wooden floors are
reminders of this classy bistro's past
as a saddler's shop. The changing
menu of regional produce has dishes
like griddled rare breed beef bernaise
and fillet of mackerel with polenta
and pesto. Tapas are also an option.
Desserts range from a choice of local
cheeses to Yorkshire curd tart. ££

Spring Espresso
45 Fossgate; tel: 07779 294149;
www.springespresso.co.uk; Mon–Fri
8am–5pm, Sat 9am–5.30pm, Sun
10am–5pm.
With a barista renowned throughout
the country, some of the best coffee in
town is found at this independent, arti-
san coffee shop. Complement this with
some scrumptious homemade cakes,
tasty soups and sandwiches, served
with crisps and salad. £

Roman and Viking York

The city played host to everyone from the Emperor Hadrian to Eric Bloodaxe – and all left their imprint on the city

York is embedded in history, and the city boasts an extraordinary range and richness of both Roman and Viking remains.

ROMAN YORK

It was in AD71 that the Romans founded York (known to them as Eboracum), whilst on a conquering raid into northern Britain. Governor Petilius Cerialis had an earth rampart and fortress erected at the confluence of the Foss and the Ouse. It grew into a 50-acre (20-hectare) fortress, with massive limestone walls, gateways and watchtowers.

Roman York must have presented an impressive sight. Two modern streets, Petergate and Stonegate, follow the Roman street pattern and some 10ft (3m) below the modern city, Roman Eboracum still lies buried with its barrack blocks, houses and bath buildings.

At the heart of the Roman city was the colonnaded forum of the legionary headquarters, now buried deep beneath the cathedral. From here Roman authority held sway over northern Britain – and at times over the whole Roman world when emperors were in residence, such as AD208, when Em-

in the Museum Gardens *(see p.72)*. But over the years countless excavations have uncovered statues, gravestones, Roman walls, towers, barrack blocks and other relics which testify to the power and status of the city. A public house in St Sampson's Square, for example, has a glass panel in the floor so visitors can look down into a Roman bathhouse. Many finds have been discovered by workmen, such as the remains of a Roman column, found beneath York Minster by builders working on the Central Tower. Even more unexpected was the discovery of a Roman sewer under Church Street.

The start of Constantine's reign might well have represented a high point for Roman York, for in the latter years of the 4th century the city gradually declined, with a decrease in trade, and a shrinking in the population. By around 410, the Romans had left York – and Britain.

VIKING YORK

Historians still debate what happened to Roman York after the legions left. The Saxons had a trading post on the riverbank (confirmed by excavations when a new hotel was built in Fishergate) and then the Vikings sailed up the Ouse – settling outside the walls of the decaying city.

The wooden walls of Viking homes were found in 1979–81 excavations in Coppergate. The moist earth helped to preserve thousands of everyday items, ranging from leather and cloth to a Viking toilet – and its contents. The Jorvik Viking Centre *(see p.44)* is based on these astonishing finds, which revealed that heather was probably used as Viking bedding, and that Viking York was an important manufacturing centre, with metalworkers, shoe-makers, carvers and cup-makers all plying their trade. It was, of course, the Vikings not the Romans who gave York its modern name – York being a corruption of Jorvik.

peror Septimius Severus established his Imperial Court here. Eboracum's importance was further emphasised in 306, when the reign of Constantine the Great began in the city: he was proclaimed emperor by his soldiers following the death of his father, Constantius. Both had been in England at the time.

Today, the only above-ground evidence of what Roman York must have looked like is the Multangular Tower

Above: a bronze statue of Constantine outside the South Transept of York Minster.
Top Left and Right: Viking York is kept alive at the Jorvik Centre. **Left**: Roman relief of Mithras found in York in the 18th century.

Tour 8

Excursion to Yorkshire Coast

Heading northeast from York, this 76 mile (122km) one- or two-day tour takes you to the lovely Yorkshire coast, taking in historic Whitby and traditional seaside town Scarborough

This excursion showcases Yorkshire's dramatically varied landscapes, taking you over the peaceful North York Moors to the coast, which is dotted with a mix of dramatic headlands, quiet bays, fishing villages, historic towns and lively resorts.

Highlights

- Kirkham Priory
- Eden Camp
- Whitby
- Robin Hood's Bay
- Scarborough

KIRKHAM PRIORY

From York, head northeast on the A64. After 15 miles (24km), a minor road leads to **Kirkham Priory ❶** (www.english-heritage.org.uk; Apr–July and Sept, Mon, Thu–Sun 10am–5pm, Aug daily 10am–6pm, Oct–Mar Sat–Sun 10am–4pm; charge). This 12th-century Augustinian monastery is now a picturesque ruin on the Derwent riverbank, but during WWII it was a training area for troops.

EDEN CAMP

Back on the A64, head towards Malton. Close by on the left is **Eden Camp ❷** (tel: 01653 697777; www.eden camp.co.uk; daily 10am–5pm; charge), a former WWII PoW camp converted to bring to life different aspects of the war in a family-friendly way.

Then take a left onto the A169 to **Pickering ❸**, a charming market town with a ruined Norman **castle**.

Left: Scarborough beach and castle.

THE YORKSHIRE COAST

If you have time for a detour, bear left before reaching Whitby and go north along the coast, on the A174, to **Staithes ❹**. Once a major fishing port, the town is famed for its link to Captain James Cook, born nearby. Its small heritage centre (tel: 01947 841454; daily 10am–5pm) is filled with information on his voyages.

Whitby

Return to **Whitby ❺**, an old whaling port, where there are more memories of Captain Cook, who trained as a seaman here and lodged with Captain John Walker in a house on the harbour, now the **Captain Cook Memorial Museum** (www.cook museumwhitby.co.uk; daily mid-Feb–Mar 11am–3pm, Apr–Oct 9.45am–5pm; charge). You'll see some of his

⑤ Dracula's Haunt

Whitby provided Bram Stoker with much of the inspiration for his Gothic horror novel *Dracula*. He supposedly came across the name 'Dracula' in a book in the local library, and the town is the scene for the first meeting between Lucy and Dracula. A memorial bench commemorates the spot where Bram Stoker admired the view of the harbour, Abbey and church. Every April and October, Whitby organises a Goth Weekend.

Above: the Abbey admired by Stoker.

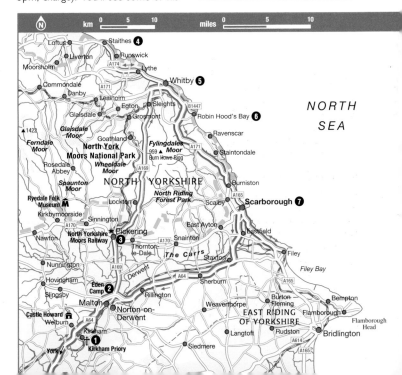

letters amongst other memorabilia. Cook sailed from Whitby on his famous voyage to Australia.

The town and harbour are cramped in a steep river valley overlooked by the ruins of the **Abbey of St Hilda** (Apr–Sept daily 10am–6pm, Oct Thu–Mon 10am–5pm, Nov–Mar Sat–Sun 10am–4pm, with exceptions; charge). Founded around AD657, the Abbey was deserted after the Dissolution and stones from it used to build a mansion, now an interactive visitor centre.

Robin Hood's Bay
South of Whitby on the A171, take the B1447 to **Robin Hood's Bay ❻**, nestled at the foot of a steep cliff road. The village has lost scores of its houses to the sea over the last two centuries. This was once a smugglers' haunt, with secret passageways and hideaways. It now attracts fossil-hunters: guided fossil walks are organised by the North Yorks Geology Trust (tel: 01947 881000).

Scarborough
Return to the A171 and south to bustling **Scarborough ❼**, a former spa town with two bays, a harbour and a castle. The South Bay has a typically brash English seafront.

At the **Rotunda Museum** (tel: 01723 353665; www.rotundamuseum.

K Railway Fun
The 18-mile (29km) North Yorkshire Moors Railway steam train route (www.nymr.co.uk) runs from Pickering to Grosmont and on some days to Whitby. Day Rover tickets allow you to get on and off to explore pretty villages such as Goathland.

Above: North Yorkshire steam train.

co.uk; Tue–Sun 10am–5pm; charge), the 19th-century creation of William Smith, father of English geology, exhibits bring to life the dinosaur coast, and there are family-friendly fossil-hunting events. Nearby, the **Art Gallery** in an Italianate villa has an eclectic collection.

The town has an enviable theatrical reputation built around Alan Ayckbourn, the local-born playwright. From Scarborough you can head south to Filey, a quieter holiday town. Nearby Flamborough Head is popular with birdwatchers. To return back to York, pick up the A64 southbound.

E Eating Out
Whitby
Green's of Whitby
13 Bridge Street; tel: 01947 600284; www.greensofwhitby.com; Mon–Fri noon–2pm, 6.30–9.30pm, Sat–Sun noon–10pm.
Seafood is a speciality, with a daily menu of local fish such as Whitby squid, scallops and sea bass. £££

Scarborough
The Green Room
138 Victoria Street; tel: 01723 501801;

www.thegreenroomrestaurant.com; Tue, Wed 5.30–9pm, Thu until 9.30pm, Fri, Sat until 10pm.
Imaginative cooking using local produce such as salmon or mackerel for starters. ££
Lanterna
33 Queen Street; tel: 01723 363616; www.lanterna-ristorante.co.uk; Mon–Sat 7–9.30pm.
Lanterna offers Italian favourites with a Piedmontese flavour: risottos, truffle dishes, as well as local fish. £££

Tour 9

Excursion around Harrogate

Heading west of York, this 35-mile (56km) one- or two-day tour takes you to the elegant spa town of Harrogate, then to the Dales and the stunning remains of Fountains Abbey

Highlights

- Knaresborough
- Harrogate
- Ripley
- Fountains Abbey and Studley Royal

You can easily reach both Knaresborough and Harrogate by train from York and do part of this tour as a day trip. However, if you wish to take in other sights, like the pretty village of Ripley and the picturesque remains of Fountains Abbey, Britain's largest monastic ruin, then you'll need a car.

This part of Yorkshire has long been on the tourist trail, and is still extremely rewarding to visit, with a wealth of historic sights, picture-perfect scenery and

Above: Knaresborough's picturesque railway viaduct crosses the River Nidd.

traditional country pubs. A popular spa town since Georgian times, Harrogate has long attracted well-heeled visitors who have come to taste its healing waters. With its wide streets and spacious swathes of smooth grassland, it provides a pleasant contrast to York's maze of ancient alleyways.

KNARESBOROUGH

Heading west from York, take the A59, passing close to the site of the battle of Marston Moor, where in 1644 the Royalists were beaten by Parliamentary forces. Continue to the historic town of **Knaresborough ❶**, which sits on the River Nidd and is topped by the ruins

Above: Harrogate's Pump Room.

of **Knaresborough Castle** (daily 11am–4pm Easter–Oct; charge).

Built by the Normans around 1100, the castle overlooks the river. It was used as a refuge by the murderers of Thomas Becket, after they had struck the clergyman down in Canterbury Cathedral, and was often visited by King John, who used the castle as a grand hunting lodge. After the Royalist defeat in the Civil War, the castle was largely destroyed – though the tower remains. Today, visitors can see the dungeons, one of the secret underground tunnels (which provided safe passage in times of siege) and an exhibition of life in a medieval castle.

Mother Shipton's Cave

Knaresborough is also famed as the birthplace of Ursula Sontheil, better known as Mother Shipton, England's most famous prophetess. She was said to have been born in 1488 in a cave by the Nidd and early in life became known for her prophecies. She is said to have predicted the Dissolution of the Monasteries, the deaths of Lady Jane Grey and Mary, Queen of Scots, the Spanish Armada and the Great Fire of London. **Mother Shipton's Cave** (tel: 01423 864000; www.mother shipton.co.uk; Apr–Oct daily 10am–5.30pm, Mar daily 10am–4.30pm, Feb

Sat–Sun 10am–5pm; charge) and the neighbouring Petrifying Well, where objects are turned to stone by the mineral-rich waters, are now visitor attractions. You can also follow a riverside walk along the Nidd.

HARROGATE

From Knaresborough, pick up the road to **Harrogate ❷**, a short drive away. This is one of the most handsome towns in England, renowned for its spa heritage, its gardens, great shops and attractive Georgian and Victorian terraces.

The **Royal Pump Room Museum** (tel: 01423 556188; www.harro

Above: Harlow Carr Garden.

gate.gov.uk, Mon–Sat 10am–5pm, Sun 2–5pm, closes 4pm Nov–Mar, Sun noon–5pm Aug; charge) gives an insight into the gilded days when thousands of people swarmed on Harrogate to take the sulphurous spa waters reputed to have healing properties. The waters tasted so bad that they spawned a thriving industry in Harrogate toffee, consumed to take away the taste of their 'cure'. You can still taste the waters today. The museum also has a permanent exhibition of ancient Egyptian treasures, which include a 5,000-year-old vase, and a sarcophagus.

For more contemporary spa treatments head to the restored **Turkish Baths and Spa** (Parliament Street; tel: 01423 556746; www.turkishbaths harrogate.co.uk) which offer spa treatments in a glorious setting *(see p.119)*.

The Mercer Art Gallery

Art-lovers should make for the **Mercer Art Gallery** (Swan Road; tel: 01423 556188; Tue–Sat 10am–5pm, Sun 2pm–5pm; free), which has around 2,000 works of art, mainly 19th- and 20th-century paintings and prints. A changing exhibition programme features works from the collection, by artists like William Powell Frith, Edward Burne-Jones and Alan Davie.

The town also has a couple of commercial art galleries. The Anstey Galleries (Swan Road; tel: 01423 500102; www.ansteygalleries.co.uk) exhibits works by contemporary artists and jewellers, while the Sutcliffe Galleries (Royal Parade, tel: 01423 562976, www.sutcliffegalleries.co.uk) specialises in 19th-century art.

Great gardens

Harrogate has some fine gardens and open spaces, including The Stray, a sweep of smooth grass on the edge of the city covered with golden daffodils in the spring. On the other side of the

F William Powell Frith

William Powell Frith (1819–1909) was one of the most popular Victorian painters; his works attracted huge crowds when they were exhibited in his day. He is known for his panoramic scenes of Victorian life, like lively crowds at Derby Day or at Paddington Station. Born near Harrogate, one of his most famous works is in the Mercer Art Gallery: *Many Happy Returns of the Day*, depicting his daughter's sixth birthday party.

Above: Frith specialised in portraits and Victorian life scenes.

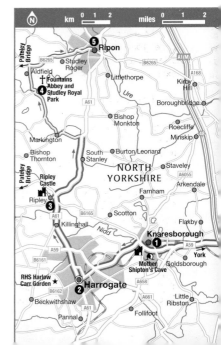

Above: Ripley Castle, family home of the Ingilbys for 28 generations.

town, close to the Pump Room, are **Valley Gardens** – English Heritage-listed gardens with mineral springs, a pavilion and extensive woodlands.

A short drive out of town, off the B6162, is **Harlow Carr Garden** (www.rhs.org.uk; daily 9.30am–6pm, Nov–Feb until 4pm; charge). This botanical garden opened in 1950 on ground that was once part of the Forest of Knaresborough. The gardens have something to offer at every time of year, though the herbaceous borders are at their best in summer. There is a popular branch of Bettys, the Yorkshire tea room, with a terrace overlooking the grounds.

RIPLEY

From Harrogate, take the A61 north to **Ripley** ❸, a neat little village of cobbled squares and stone cottages reminiscent of Alsace-Lorraine, after the French region took the fancy of Sir William Amcotts Ingilby on his travels. The Ingilby family has lived in Ripley

Ⓚ Family Fun

Ripley Castle hosts a variety of events throughout the year, providing great family entertainment. Past events have included falconry displays, carriage-driving trials and classic car rallies, as well as an annual agricultural show in August featuring local handicrafts and sheep dog trials. The gardens have also provided a spectacular backdrop to Shakespeare plays and summer evening concerts. Details on www.ripleycastle.co.uk.

Above: classic cars on show in the grounds of Ripley Castle.

for 700 years and their home, **Ripley Castle** (tel: 01423 770152; www.ripleycastle.co.uk; castle: Easter–Oct daily 11am–3pm, Mar, Nov Tue, Thu, Sat–Sun 11am–3pm, Dec–Feb Sat–Sun 11am–3pm, guided tours only; gardens: daily 9am–4.30, 5pm; charge). Tours of the castle reveal suitably grand rooms, armour from the Civil War, and a 'priest's hole' – the secret room where the Catholic priest Francis Ingilby hid during anti-Catholic raids in Elizabeth I's time. The Inglibys have a fascinating family history – they were, for example, related to many of the Gunpowder Plot conspirators, while Jane Ingilby, a royalist, is said to have once held Oliver Cromwell hostage at pistol point in the castle's library.

The **castle gardens** are delightful, and include 4 acres (1.6 hectares) of Victorian walled gardens, as well as a kitchen garden filled with rare herbs and spices. The pleasure grounds burst into glorious displays of snowdrops in early spring, followed by buttery yellow daffodils and delicate primroses. You can wander down to the lakeside, where fallow deer graze, and children can let off steam on the play trail.

Do make time to stroll around the village of Ripley. The 15th-century church of All Saints features a grim series of marks on one wall, said to have been made by Cromwell's troops as they executed Royalist soldiers following the battle of Marston Moor. The village also has a famous ice-cream shop.

FOUNTAINS ABBEY AND STUDLEY ROYAL

From Ripley, go north on the A61. Then either bear left on minor roads, or turn left in Ripon onto the B6265, off which is the World Heritage Site of **Fountains Abbey and Studley Royal** ❹ (tel: 01765 608888; www.nationaltrust.org.uk; daily 10am–6pm; deer park: daily all year; charge).

Fountains Abbey

In 1132, 13 Benedictine monks split from the powerful community at St Mary's Abbey in York, which they deemed not devout enough, and established a new monastery here, in the tranquil rural location they craved. A few years later they became Cistercian monks, an austere order demanding long periods of silence, a frugal regime and the wearing of harsh white robes. The Abbey grew rapidly, with the help of a large community of lay brothers, who carried out routine tasks on behalf of the monks and also tended the vast flocks of sheep – turning it into one of the richest religious houses in England.

Following Henry VIII's Dissolution of the Monasteries, Fountains fell into rapid decline. Glass and lead were stripped from the building, and many of the stones used to create the Jacobean mansion of **Fountains Hall**, which has an impressive minstrel gallery open to the public (part of the Hall is now used to provide National Trust holiday apartments).

The Abbey passed through the hands of various owners until, in the 18th century, it was purchased by William Aislabie, who landscaped the ruins to provide a picturesque sight that could

Above: Fountains Abbey.

Nidderdale Museum

Visitors with children might enjoy a diversion to Pateley Bridge, west of Ripley, home to the Nidderdale Museum (tel: 01423 711225, www. nidderdalemuseum.com; Easter–Oct daily 1.30–4.30pm Nov–Easter, Sat–Sun 1.30–4.30pm; charge). It's devoted to the rural life of the dales, with exhibits on everything from agriculture to clothing. There's a recreated Victorian parlour, a school-room and a general store.

Above: step back in time at the Nidderdale Museum.

be viewed from the water garden of Studley Royal. Strolling round the Abbey ruins today gives you a sense of the scale of the original building. These are the largest monastic ruins in Britain and you can still see the cellarium, where the lay brothers ate and slept (now home to several protected species of bat), and the cloisters, where the monks would exercise and meditate.

Below: the beautifully laid-out Studley Royal Water Gardens.

Studley Royal
Studley Royal Water Gardens (same hours and prices as abbey) were created in the 18th century by John Aislabie, a wealthy but disgraced MP. He devoted himself to creating a spectacular water garden in the valley of the River Skell – with vast expanses of smooth water, geometric shapes and a smattering of statues and follies. As you stroll around the gardens you can see the neoclassical Temple of Piety, the Gothic Octagon Tower and the Temple of Fame – used as a picnic spot by the Georgians. There are also grottoes, cascades and a rustic bridge – made to look older. When John Aislabie died, his son William extended the landscaped area, adding the romantic feature of Fountains Abbey to the vistas.

St Mary's Church
Also within the grounds is **St Mary's Church** (noon–4pm Easter–Sept), commissioned in 1870 by the Marchioness of Ripon to commemorate her murdered brother. The church was designed by William Burges, and is a fine example of the High Victorian Gothic style. Its richly decorated interior has carved parrots above the choir stalls and an organ case designed to resemble a medieval house. The site is

so large that it could easily make a full day's outing, especially if you also take a stroll through the woodland or follow one of the marked trails. There's a café and a visitor centre too.

RIPON

Leaving Fountains Abbey, pick up the B6265 east to **Ripon ❺**. This pleasant market town has a **cathedral** (www. riponcathedral.org.uk; daily 8.30am– 6pm; free) originating in the 7th century. Today's building is the fourth church to stand on this site, but you can see the crypt of the first church, created by St Wilfrid in AD672. The cathedral also has an Art Nouveau pulpit and 15th-century carvings in the choir – the one depicting a griffin chasing a rabbit down a hole is thought to have inspired Lewis Carroll in his *Alice's Adventures in Wonderland*. His father was once the cathedral's canon, and Carroll visited many times. The cathedral also has associations with the war poet Wilfred Owen, who visited it in 1918, before being sent back to France, where he was killed. Owen composed two poems in Ripon. From Ripon take the A61 back to Harrogate, and then York.

Ⓔ Eating Out

Harrogate

The Pine Marten
Otley Road; tel: 01423 709999; www. thepinemarten.com; food served daily noon–9.30pm, Sun until 8.30pm.
This popular contemporary country pub, just outside Harrogate on the road to Harlow Carr Garden, offers sharing plates of Mediterranean-influenced food, as well as pizzas, salads, pasta dishes and steaks. ££

The Tannin Level
5 Raglan Street; tel: 01423 560595; www.tanninlevel.co.uk; Mon–Thu noon–9pm, Fri–Sat until 9.30pm, Sun until 8pm.
This popular wine bar-bistro serves local produce in a relaxed atmosphere. It's essentially modern British food with a Mediterranean twist. The menu changes regularly but includes dishes like salmon fish fingers with chips and maple-roasted belly pork. Desserts might include treacle tart with whisky-soaked prunes and a classic sticky toffee pudding. £££

Van Zeller
8 Montpellier Street; tel: 01423 508762; www.vanzellerrestaurants. co.uk; Tue–Sat noon–2pm, 6–10pm, Sun noon–2.30pm.
Boasting two AA rosettes, this restaurant in Harrogate's chic Montpellier district offers fine food in minimal surroundings. Main courses include quail roasted with black pudding, wild trout with summer vegetables and wild turbot in a parmesan and hazelnut crust. And for dessert, there's a chocolate delice and a strawberry and vanilla parfait. You can also opt for the 10-course tasting menu. £££

Ripley

The Boar's Head
Ripley Village; tel: 01423 771888; www.boarsheadripley.co.uk; Mon–Sat noon–2.30pm, 7–9pm, Sun 9am–8pm.
This former coaching inn, part of the Ripley Castle estate, has a formal restaurant serving seasonal produce and a more informal Bistro. £££

Pateley Bridge

The Yorke Arms
Ramsgill-in-Nidderdale, nr Pateley Bridge; tel: 01423 755243; www.yorke-arms.co.uk; daily lunch and dinner.
This Michelin-starred, 18th-century coaching house grows many of its own ingredients and features local produce like Nidderdale lamb. Also on the menu are saddle of red deer with kidneys and slow-cooked shoulder of lamb. The Sunday lunch menu includes a traditional sirloin of beef served with Yorkshire pudding. Booking advisable. £££

Excursion to James Herriot Country

This 50-mile (80km) full-day tour takes you to some of the most dramatic scenery in the North York Moors, much of which is now better known as James Herriot Country

The thriving market town of Thirsk, immortalised as 'Darrowby' in the James Herriot books, makes a pleasant first stop on this tour which then bears east, taking you onto the North York Moors – the heather covered moorland that is sliced by deep dales and dotted with ancient abbeys, farms and pretty villages.

Highlights

- Thirsk
- Sutton Bank
- Shandy Hall
- Byland Abbey
- Helmsley Castle
- Rievaulx Abbey

THIRSK

From York, take the A19 northwest to **Thirsk ❶**, better known to readers of the James Herriot veterinary books as Darrowby. James Herriot was the literary name of Yorkshire vet Alf Wight (1916–95), whose humorous books describing his working life and the local characters he met brought him unexpected fame – especially when they were translated in the 1980s into the TV series *All Creatures Great and Small*. His depictions of the landscape immortalised the area for millions of readers and sparked a Herriot tourism industry.

Left: the superb view from Sutton Bank praised by James Herriot (above).

The World of James Herriot (Kirkgate; tel: 01845 524234; www. worldofjamesherriot.org; daily Mar–Oct 10am–5pm, Nov–Feb until 4pm; charge) is set in 'Skeldale House', the building where Alf Wight ran his veterinary practice, and has rooms set out just as they were in the 1940s when he worked here.

St Mary's Church was built in the 15th century, in perpendicular Gothic style, with a soaring 80ft (24m) tower. It was here, in 1941, that Alf Wight married Joan Danby (Helen Alderson in the books). The town also has a small **museum** in the house that was the birthplace of Thomas Lord, the founder of Lord's cricket ground.

SUTTON BANK

From Thirsk, take the A170 east, where the road soon climbs steeply to **Sutton Bank ❷**, a dramatic escarpment rising above the surrounding countryside, offering some of the finest views in Britain – often mentioned in the James Herriot books. It is now home to the **National Park Visitor Centre** (tel: 01845 597428; Mar–Oct daily 10am–5pm, Nov–Feb Sat–Sun 10.30am–4.30pm, with exceptions), where there are displays on the local landscape, a bird-feeding station, a cycle centre and a tea room. The centre also has booklets and information on easy walks from Sutton Bank, including one that runs along the edge of the escarpment to the famous Kilburn White Horse etched into the hillside.

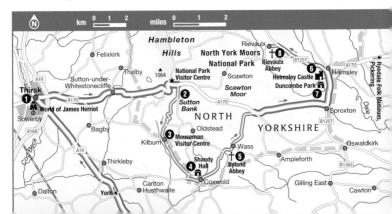

KILBURN

Continue east on the A170 for a short distance, before branching off to **Kilburn**. This village was once home to the accomplished woodcarver Robert 'Mousey' Thompson (1876–1955), famed for the trademark mouse he carved on his pieces. Using English oak, he produced furniture and wooden items inspired by 17th-century English works. His distinctive pieces began appearing in churches all over the country, and you will often find a mouse hidden on a wooden pew. His workshop continues to produce 'Mouseman' carving today. The **Mouseman Visitor Centre** ❸ (tel: 01347 869102; www.robertthompsons.co.uk; Easter–Oct daily 10am–5pm, Nov–Dec Wed–Sun 11am–4pm) in the village has a showroom displaying Thompson's work.

SHANDY HALL

From Kilburn, minor roads lead south to the village of Coxwold, the location for **Shandy Hall** ❹ (tel: 01347 868465; www.laurencesternetrust.org.uk; house: May–Sept Wed 2–4.30pm, Sun 2.30–4.30pm; gardens: May–Sept Sun–Fri 11am–4.30pm; charge), which in the 1760s was home to the writer Laurence Sterne, author of the humorous and eccentric *The Life and Opinions of Tristram Shandy*. The house is both a

Above: Helmsley Castle.

home and a museum containing a comprehensive collection of first editions of his books and letters.

BYLAND ABBEY

From Coxwold, take a minor road running northeast to **Byland Abbey** ❺ (tel: 01347 868614; www.english-heritage.org.uk; July–Aug daily 10am–6pm, Apr–June, Sept–Oct Thu–Mon 10am–6pm, Nov–Mar Sat–Sun 10am–4pm; charge). This ruined abbey was once home to over 200 monks and lay brothers of the Cistercian order. The rose window is thought to have provided the model for that of York Minster.

HELMSLEY

From the abbey go north to join the A170 and turn right for the pretty village of Helmsley. **Helmsley Castle** ❻ (tel: 01439 770442; www.english-heritage.org.uk; Apr–Sept daily 10am–6pm, Oct Thu–Mon 10am–5pm, Nov–Mar Sat–Sun 10am–4pm; charge) was begun in 1120 and fortified in the 14th and 15th centuries.

Above: the Mouseman Visitor Centre keeps Robert Thompson's 'Mouseman' carving tradition alive.

Duncombe Park

On the edge of Helmsley, **Duncombe Park** ❼ (tel: 01439 772625, www.duncombepark.com; gardens and parklands: Sun–Fri 10am–5pm; charge) is a grand stately home (not open to the public) set in extensive grounds. The estate was purchased by wealthy banker Sir Charles Duncombe, who built a Baroque mansion in 1713. This was rebuilt following a fire in the 19th century. It remained the home of the Duncombes until the death of the Second Earl of Feversham in WWI. It was then let out as a boarding school, but in the 1980s the then Lord and Lady Feversham restored it and made it into their family home again. In 2013 an International Centre for Birds of Prey (www.icbp-duncombe.org; Feb–Dec daily 10am–5.30pm) opened within the grounds, which houses the largest collection of raptors in the north of England. There are flying demonstrations every day.

RIEVAULX ABBEY

Leaving Helmsley, pick up the B1257 running north, then turn off on a minor road to the romantic ruins of **Rievaulx Abbey** ❽ (tel: 01439 798228; www.english-heritage.org.uk; Easter–Sept daily 10am–6pm, Oct until 5pm, Nov–Easter Sat–Sun 10am–4pm, with exceptions; charge). Founded in 1132 by St Bernard of Clairvaux, the Abbey grew into one of England's wealthiest medieval monasteries and the first Cistercian monastery in the north. Ecclesiastical bliss did not prevail however, as the monks disputed land rights with those of nearby Byland Abbey – leading to some monastic engineering works to divert the course of the River Rye, which was the boundary between their properties.

Return to the A170 back to Thirsk to pick up the A19 down to York.

Above: Rievaulx is one of the most atmospheric of England's abbey ruins.

Ⓔ Eating Out

Thirsk

Crown and Anchor
138 Front Street, Sowerby, nr Thirsk; tel: 01845 522448; www.crownandanchorsowerby.co.uk; Tue–Sat lunch and dinner, Mon dinner, Sun lunch. This attractive village pub serves a good range of traditional food, from tasty sandwiches to popular Sunday roasts, as well as continental beers. £

Golden Fleece
Market Place; tel: 01845 523108; www.goldenfleecehotel.com; daily breakfast, lunch, afternoon tea and dinner. This former coaching inn is perfect for relaxed bar meals or more formal dining in the restaurant, where local produce is generally on the menu. ££

Helmsley

Feversham Arms; tel: 01439 770766; www.fevershamarmshotel.com; daily 6.45–9.30pm.
The restaurant in this former coaching inn, now a four-star hotel, offers local produce such as roast sea bream with chorizo tortellini or duck with haricot blanc and Morteau sausage. Afternoon tea is available between 2pm and 4pm in the cosy hotel lounge. £££

Tour 11

Excursion to Castle Howard

North from York on the A64 it's a 15-mile (24km) journey to Castle Howard; plan for a full-day excursion

Visitor Information

Tel: 01653 648333; www.castle howard.co.uk; house: daily mid-Mar–Oct and end Nov–mid Dec 11am–4pm (last admission); garden: daily 10am–5.30pm until 4pm in winter; shops: daily 10am–5pm.

Above and Below: Castle Howard lies on stunning landscaped grounds.

Yorkshire has more than its fair share of fine houses, but nothing surpasses **Castle Howard ❶**, one of the most stunning stately homes in Britain. The 18th-century house, set in 1,000 acres (400 hectares) of picture-perfect grounds, was chosen as the location for the opulent 1981 TV version of Evelyn Waugh's classic novel *Brideshead Revisited*, and featured again in the 2008 movie version. As well as visiting the house, you can shop for plants and food in the stable courtyard, and enjoy walks in the parkland and woods. Youngsters will enjoy the lakeside adventure playground.

VANBRUGH'S CREATION

Castle Howard stands on a hilltop overlooking a landscaped lake. Designed by Sir John Vanburgh for the Third Earl of Carlisle, this is country living on the grand scale – a marbled, domed entrance hall, staterooms lavishly furnished with Sheraton and Chippendale and Old Masters on the walls.

Work on the house began in 1699. At the time, Vanburgh was a dramatist and had never before designed a property. He was later assisted by Nicholas Hawksmoor, the great church architect. The house was so vast and so palatial that it took over 100 years to be completed. It was badly damaged by a fire in 1940 and Vanbrugh's distinctive dome in the Great Hall was destroyed. This was rebuilt in the 1960s; it reaches 70ft (21m) and is exuberantly painted inside with images of the figures of the zodiac. More restoration work was made possible when the house was chosen as the location for *Brideshead Revisited*.

FINE ARTWORKS

The rooms of the house are filled with artistic treasures. There is fine porcelain by Meissen, Sèvres and Crown Derby, and paintings by artists such as Canaletto, George Stubbs and Sir Joshua Reynolds. The most famous painting in the collection is Thomas Gainsborough's work *Girl with Pigs*. In the private chapel, you can see an embroidered screen by William Morris and stained glass by Edward Burne-Jones.

THE GROUNDS

The lakes in the grounds were created in the 18th century. They are surrounded by smooth grasslands and adorned by ornamental structures such as the Temple of the Four Winds, originally designed by Vanburgh and modelled on Palladio's Villa Rotonda in Vicenza. It was a place for relaxation, appreciation of the views and as somewhere to take refreshment. There's a cellar beneath it, where servants stored food. The mausoleum in the grounds, designed

by Hawksmoor, still serves as a burial place for the Howard family. There is also a woodland garden and a walled garden with an ornamental kitchen garden. From the lakeside adventure playground, you can take a boat trip on the lake to spot wildlife (summer only).

The renovated Stable Courtyard at the entrance houses a café, a farm shop selling local food and ales, a bookshop and a gift shop. There's a changing programmed of events at Castle Howard, ranging from wine-tasting evenings to specialist courses in photography or landscape painting.

Ⓔ Eating Out

Courtyard Café
Tel: 01653 648634; daily 10am–5pm, 10am–5pm winter weekdays. Located in the Stable Courtyard by the ticket office, the Castle's café is open to non-ticket-holders too. It serves bistro-style seasonal food, including meat from the estate farm shop, and has both indoor and outdoor seating. ££

Fitzroy Room
Same opening times as the house. In the house itself, this self-service café on the ground floor, serves cakes, sandwiches and hot meals. ££

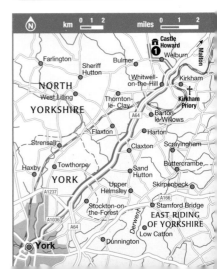

Travel Tips

Active Pursuits

If walking around York's superbly preserved City Walls or along the riverbank isn't enough exercise for you, there are plenty of other opportunities for getting active – both around the city and in the surrounding countryside. In fact, with the gloriously unspoilt landscapes of the North York Moors and the Yorkshire Dales, just a short drive away, you're really spoilt for choice.

WALKING

With 1,400 miles (2,253km) of footpaths, the North York Moors National Park (www.northyorkmoors.org.uk; see p.62) offers walks for all abilities. There are easy routes that the whole family could do, more energetic rambles that will get the lungs working, and strenuous hikes for those who like to test themselves.

There are far too many routes to mention here, but some easy walks include strolls along Sutton Bank, which provide immensely rewarding views; a 2¾-mile (4.4km) walk from Glaisdale to Egton Bridge and a 3-mile (5km) walk along a section of disused

Preceding Pages, Above and Below: there's no shortage of walks in the York countryside.

railway line, through the Esk Valley to the hamlet of Beck Hole.

If you're after a longer walk there's a 6½-mile (10.5km) walk from Old-stead to Byland Abbey, and then on to see the remains of Mount Snever Observatory, built in 1838 to commemorate Queen Victoria's coronation. Experienced walkers could challenge themselves by following the Hambleton Hills Mosaic Walk, a 36-mile (58km) walk around the western corner of the National Park or the long distance Cleveland Way (www.nationaltrail.co.uk), which stretches for some 110 miles (1,767km) from Helmsley all the way to Filey Brigg on the coast. The trail takes approximately nine days to complete.

Above: paraglider taking off over the Yorkshire countryside.

CYCLING

Cyclists, like walkers, have plenty of options in and around York. The best known long-distance route is the Moor to Sea Cycle Route (www.moortoseacycle.net), which extends for around 100 miles (161km) and easily divides into nine separate stretches. The White Rose Route is another cycle route, running for 123 miles (198 km) between Hull and Middlesborough. It takes in part of the western section of the North York Moors National Park. For more information visit www.sustrans.org.uk. There are shorter routes to cover, in forests and along disused railway lines, in the National Park – details available from Park Visitor Centres. Dalby Forest, for instance, has graded mountain bike routes and a skills area, as well as bike hire.

🅕 Spectator Sports

York attracts thousands of visitors to its horse races, held at Knavesmire (www.yorkracecourse.co.uk) with flat racing from May to October. Flat racing also takes place at Thirsk (www.thirskracecourse.net) between April and September, while Ripon Racecourse (www.ripon-races.co.uk) hosts races from April to September, with a special Children's Day in August.

Cricket fans will be pleased to know that Yorkshire Cricket Club (www.yorkshireccc.com) at Headingley, Leeds, is a short drive from York – hosting both domestic and international fixtures.

Above: horse racing.

GLIDING

Those wanting to get a bird's eye view over the Yorkshire countryside could go gliding at Yorkshire Gliding Club (tel: 01845 597237, www.ygc.co.uk). Based at Sutton Bank, the club offers trial lessons, as well as one- and five-day courses.

GOLF

Keen golfers itching to get out onto the greens will be spoilt for choice with a number of 18- and 9-hole courses within an hour's drive of York. Fulford Golf Club (tel: 01904 413579, www.fulfordgolfclub.co.uk) is just on the outskirts of the city, a couple of miles from the centre, by the university. It's an 18-hole course which accepts visitors with a handicap certificate from Monday to Friday. It's noted as the place where, in 1981, golfer Bernhard Langer played a shot from the branches of an ash tree.

York Golf Range is at Towthorpe, about 6 miles (9.5km) north of the city centre (tel: 01904 499275; www.yorkgolfrange.co.uk), and has a 9-hole course and a driving range. Lessons can also be booked, for juniors as well as adults. Not far away, at Strensall, is York's oldest golf club, York Golf Club (tel: 01904 499800, www.yorkgolfclub.co.uk). Founded in 1890, it moved to this location in 1904.

Northwest of the city, off the A19 to Thirsk, the Forest of Galtres Golf Club (tel: 01904 769400, www.forestofgaltres.co.uk) is a parkland 18-hole course with a driving range. Five-day and seven-day memberships are available.

HORSE RIDING

The North York Moors National Park has an extensive network of bridleways, as well as concessionary bridleways like the former Scarborough to Whitby railway. For those with their own horse, the Park authority has a horse rider's guide (ask at the Visitor's Centre for details).

A number of riding centres offer lessons and treks. Boltby Pony Trekking and Trail Riding Centre near Thirsk (01845 537392, www.boltbytrekking.

Below: pony trekking on the North York Moors.

Above: Yorkshire provides some great rivers for kayaking.

special children's 'learn about ponies' morning sessions, as well as longer residential and non-residential courses.

WATERSPORTS

Those wanting to try their hand at watersports such as dinghy sailing, canoeing and kayaking should check out Allerthorpe Lakeland Park (tel: 01759 301444; www.allerthorpelakelandpark. co.uk) on the A1079, 14 miles southeast of York; they offer courses and instruction for adults and juniors. If you prefer to have a go at surfing, then Scarborough Surf School (tel: 01723 585585; www.scarboroughsurfschool. co.uk), based at Cayton Bay, offers instruction for beginners and novices, as well as those wanting to improve their technique. They also hire out surf boards and wetsuits.

co.uk) does a range of introductory sessions lasting from 30-minute tasters to two-hour and whole-day treks, as well as two-day treks for more experienced riders. Friars Hill Stables (tel: 01751 432758, www.friarshillstables. co.uk) at Sinnington have an indoor school and offer a range of lessons and accompanied hacks. They also run

In York itself, Yearsley Swimming Pool, Haxby Road (tel: 01904 552424) is a six-lane Edwardian pool that has been recently restored and is open to the public for swimming sessions.

Fun for Kids

Kids over 10 years of age will love the Go Ape adventure centre (tel: 0845 643 9215; www.goape.co.uk) at Dalby Forest, Thornton-le-Dale, near Pickering. It's a forest adventure obstacle course with ladders, walkways, bridges and zip wires.

Above: At Go Ape, kids can swing through the tree canopy and get a real adrenalin rush – all safely strapped into a harness.

Themed Holidays

York and its surrounding area offer a number of themed holidays, where you can pick up or refine your skills at the same time as enjoy the local area. The golf courses, trekking and riding centres, sailing and surf schools mentioned in the Active Pursuits section all offer opportunities for themed breaks, but here are a few more suggestions that might encourage you to spend a little longer in Yorkshire.

ART

Hazlewood Castle (tel: 0808 178 7666; www.hazlewood-castle.co.uk) organises classes in watercolours amidst stunning surroundings, 15 miles (24km) southwest of York. Courses for beginners and more experienced painters are held in the castle's State Drawing room, on the lawns and in the courtyard. One- and two-night stays are available that include expert tuition from artist Anita Bowerman, whose influences include Turner, Monet and Whistler; her instruction incorporates techniques used by these artists.

COOKERY

The annual Food and Drink Festival (see p.41) might whet your appetite for more formal cooking tuition in the city.

The Cooking Rooms (tel: 01904 500 700; www.thecookingrooms.com) is a cookery school based at Clifton Moor, just a couple of miles from the city centre. There's a purpose-built kitchen and local chefs and instructors run classes ranging from master classes in specific techniques to essential skills of cookery. You can learn about fish, Italian cuisine, Indian food, cooking game, patisserie, preserving fruit and more. There are also classes for children aged 8–12 and 14–17.

SPA HOLIDAYS

Pampering spa breaks are increasingly popular. In York itself, the lovely Middlethorpe Hotel and Spa (tel: 01904 641241; www.middlethorpe.com) has a spa with a pool for the use of its residents, which offers treatments ranging from Espa aromatherapy facials to salt and oil body scrubs and relaxing Indian head massages. Non-residents can take advantage of full- and half-day packages which allow them to use the facilities too.

The new Cedar Court Grand Hotel, located near York Railway Station (tel: 01904 380038; www.cedarcourtgrand. co.uk) has a wonderful spa downstairs,

Below: the stunning, mosaic-tiled Turkish Baths in Harrogate.

with a 14m-pool and five treatment rooms, including one double room where two people can have their treatments done at the same time. It offers one-day and overnight spa breaks.

Harrogate
Harrogate, of course, is the quintessential spa town. A spa break here no longer means that you have to take the sulphurous waters each morning as the Victorians did – although you can step back in time at the beautifully restored Turkish Baths (tel: 01423 556746, www.turkishbathsharrogate.co.uk) on Parliament Street. The baths have a steam room, after which you take a chilly dip in the plunge pool, then go through three interconnecting rooms: a Tepidarium (warm), Calidarium (hot) and Laconium (hottest) before cooling down in a relaxation room.

The Turkish Baths also offer a range of relaxing treatments including facials, massages and body treatments. You could try a chocolate body wrap, hot-stone therapy, reflexology or a mud detoxing treatment.

Practical Information

GETTING THERE
By car
York is about 4 hours from London, 1½ hours from Manchester, 2 hours from Newcastle-upon-Tyne and 4 hours from Edinburgh.

The M1 motorway from London reaches Leeds 24 miles (40km) from York and continues as the A1 (M) to Newcastle. Bramham crossroads (Junction 44) on the A1 (M), some 12 miles (20km) west of York, is the city's main link with the motorway network. The approach to York from here is by the A64 which is all dual carriageway. The cross Pennine M62, which leads to Manchester, runs some 20 miles (32 km) south of the city and it can be reached either via the A1 or by a much slower route through Selby or Howden.

For local radio travel information, BBC Radio York is on 828 kHz MW, 95.5 MHz VHF; independent Minster FM is on 104.7 VHF.

By coach
National Express runs a direct coach service between London and York four times every day, as well as regular

Above: York is easily reached by train.

services from other main towns in the UK. Though slower, it is much cheaper than travelling by train. The journey from London takes a minimum of 4½ hours when you travel directly. The bus terminal in York is by the railway station. To book, tel: 08717 818178, www.nationalexpress.com

By train
Fast Intercity trains link York with London and Scotland. There is a regu-

lar service between York and London with the journey time between 1hr 50 minutes and 2hrs 20 minutes. Trains leave London from King's Cross station (tel: 08457 484950, www.nationalrail.co.uk).

Trains from York to Scarborough, Filey and Bridlington on the coast run regularly, and around six trains an hour go to Leeds.

Other useful rail companies include Cross Country Trains (www.crosscountrytrains.co.uk), First Transpennine Express (www.tpexpress.co.uk) and Grand Central (www.grandcentralrail.co.uk). York Railway Station is only a few minutes from the centre of the city but you might want to take advantage of the taxi rank in the portico, or the car rental agency.

By air

The nearest airports to York are Leeds-Bradford (northwest of Leeds) some 25 miles (40km) from York (tel: 0871 288 2288, www.leedsbradfordairport.co.uk) and Robin Hood Airport in Sheffield, 35 miles (55km) from York (tel: 0871 220 2210, www.robinhoodairport.com).

A twice-hourly train shuttle service operates from York to Manchester Airport (www.tpexpress.co.uk). For information on flights to and from the airport, tel: 08712 710711, www.manchesterairport.co.uk.

GETTING AROUND

York is a 'walkable' city and maps are available in Tourist Information Centres (see p.122). Open-top bus tours also offer a hop-on and hop-off service. City Sightseeing Tours (01904 634296, www.city-sightseeing.co.uk) run all year. Tickets can be bought at the Tourist Office or from the driver and are valid for 24 hours from time of purchase. Tickets also allow some discounts to a handful of city sites. In high season, buses run every 15–30 minutes between 9am and 5.30pm (Nov–Feb 9.30am–3.30pm).

Going Green

York has a large pedestrianised zone in the city centre, which restricts vehicles during the day, so it is a great city for walkers and cyclists. As part of the i-Travel York initiative, York Council is aiming to increase levels of cycling by 20 per cent and walking by 10 per cent by 2016, and is also working towards increasing bus usage

Below: cycling is increasingly popular in the city centre.

Above: York sightseeing bus.

by 18 per cent by 2015. Specifically targeting the northern quadrant of the city, where there are high numbers of short car trips, this should have a big impact on congestion. A cycle route map is available to download from www.york.gov.uk, or at the Tourist Information Centre. York Council Walking and Cycling Officer, tel: 01904 551550.

Driving

Narrow, winding medieval streets never make for ideal driving conditions and York has these in abundance. In addition, much of the city centre is pedestrianised (at least during the day), there are one-way systems in operation and parking charges are high so driving within the city isn't recommended for visitors. York is compact anyway, so easily negotiated on foot – although travellers with disabilities may find the narrow, cobbled streets hard to negotiate. The surrounding countryside is suited to driving; in fact many areas are hard to reach without one, so hiring a vehicle is worthwhile.

Car parks

It is best to use one of the five park-and-ride schemes: from Askham Bar on the A64 southern approach to the city; at Rawcliffe Bar on the western section of the city bypass; at Grimston Bar off the eastern section; at the Designer Outlet off the southern section close to the A19; and at Monks Cross on the Malton Road northeast of the city. Parking is free, though of course there is a charge for using the frequent bus service into the city centre.

If you really need to park closer there are car parks in Union Terrace, outside Monk Bar, at Foss Bank, St George's Field, Marygate and the Castle Car Park – if you can get in. There is multi-storey car parking at the Shambles Car Park in Garden Place and at the Piccadilly Car Park. Charges for all the central car parks are by the hour and a long stay can be very expensive, so much so that a phone line has been set up to accept payment via credit card. After all few people have enough pocket change for a day's parking in York. If you are staying in the centre, it's best to leave your car parked at the hotel or guesthouse for the duration of your stay. For park- and-ride enquiries, tel: 01904 551400.

Car rental

Car rental firms include:
Europcar, Station Road, tel: 0871 384 3458, www.europcar.co.uk, Hertz, Station Road, tel: 0843 309 3082, www. hertz.co.uk, Avis, Station Road, tel: 0844 544 6117, www.avis.co.uk, Enterprise, Foss Island Rd, tel: 01904 623000, www.enterprise.co.uk.

Buses

Bus services in York are run by a number of different companies (suburban and city services) and offer a range of discounted tickets such as all day, weekly or monthly that give you unlimited travel (www.itravelyork. info/buses). Excursions are run to nearby towns and villages (York Pullman Bus Company, tel: 01904 622992, www.yorkpullmanbus.co.uk). Another popular service is the Moorsbus (tel: 01845 597000) that connects York with Whitby and other seaside towns via numerous towns and villages in the North York Moors National Park.

Taxis

Taxis can't be hailed on the street but there are taxi ranks outside the train station and the City Art Gallery (nights only). Otherwise you must ring for them to collect you. Station Taxis, tel: 01904 623332; www.york stationtaxis.co.uk. Streamline Taxis, tel: 01904 656565. Fleetway Taxis: 01904 365365; www.fleetways.co.uk.

Cycle hire

You can hire bicycles from Cycle Heaven, York Station, tel: 01904 622701; www.cycle-heaven.co.uk, or Scoot, tel: 01904 720003; www.scootcycling holidays.co.uk. Scoot offers free collection and delivery to your hotel.

FACTS FOR THE VISITOR

Disabled travellers

York's narrow, sometimes cobbled, streets can be hard to negotiate for visitors with disabilities – and many of the city's ancient buildings have inaccessible areas. However scooters, and both powered and manual wheelchairs, are available for hire from Shopmobility, level 2, Piccadilly Car Park, tel: 01904 679222. Orange badge holders may park free in all city council car parks (except the Shambles). An increasing number of city buses are suitable for wheelchairs too.

Emergencies

For police, ambulance and fire brigade, tel: 999.
York Police Station, Fulford Road, tel: (non emergencies) 101.
York Hospital is at Wiggington Road, tel: 01904 631313.

Above: signpost outside the Minster.

Opening times

York is 'open' all year round but visiting for most of the stately homes in the vicinity is seasonal, usually Easter to October. Many of York's city-centre shops are open on Sundays, particularly during the summer. Main trading hours are Mon–Sat 9am–5.30pm, though many premises may stay open a little later, especially on Thursdays.

Tourist information

The city tourist information centre has a range of guidebooks, maps and information. The staff will also take bookings for accommodation, tours and excursions. You will find it at: 1 Museum St, close to York Minster (tel: 01904 550099; www.visityork. org; Mon–Sat 9am–5pm, July–Aug until 5.30pm, Sun 10am–4pm).

York Pass

Valid for up to three days, the York Pass gives free entry to over 30 popular places of interest in York, as well as attractions in the surrounding area such as the Yorkshire Air Museum and Eden Camp, Castle Howard, Harewood House and North Yorkshire Moors Railway. Passes last one, two, three or six days.

You can buy the pass online at www.yorkpass.com or tel: 01904 550 099. They are also for sale at the tourist information centres.

Sightseeing tours

Open-top buses tour parts of the city that can still be reached on wheels, hop-on and hop-off, all day *(see p. 120)*.

Walking guided tours run by the Association of Voluntary Guides start from Exhibition Square, tel; 01904 550098. There are also Viking Walks, tel: 07508 015610, and themed walks (Roman York, Secret York, etc.) with Yorkwalk, tel: 01904 622303; www. yorkwalk.co.uk.

ⓕ Gay and Lesbian

York does not have a great number of specifically gay/lesbian pubs and clubs. For further information contact York Pride, www.yorkpride. org.uk or York Gay Switchboard tel: 01904 612828. There is an annual Lesbian Music, Arts and Comedy Festival in the city.

A fair number of ghost-walk organisers compete for passing customers. Look out for the Original Ghost Walk of York, tel: 01904 764222; the Ghost Hunt of York, www.ghosthunt.co.uk and Ghost Trail, tel: 01904 633276; www.ghosttrail.co.uk.

Postal services

The main post office is situated at 22 Lendal (Mon–Sat 9am–5.30pm). The regional sorting office is located in Leeman Road near the Marble Arch Railway Bridge and is useful for late-night posting of urgent mail. Tel: 08457 223344.

Above: tour bus waiting for its passengers outside York Minster.

Accommodation

York has a wide variety of accommodation available, ranging from luxury hotels and international hotel chains to smaller bed and breakfasts, guesthouses and some good-quality self-catering accommodation, which can be a good option for those staying more than a couple of days. You can even stay in a working convent (www.bar-convent.org.uk).

Most visitors want to stay within the City Walls, especially if they are only staying one night, but there are some good options just a short distance outside which are well worth considering (and which may be slightly cheaper). There is also reasonably priced seasonal accommodation in the halls and self-catering flats of York University, situated on the campus a couple of miles from the centre (www.yorkrooms.com). Regular buses run into the city.

In summer, particularly during race meetings and festivals, it is safer to book accommodation well ahead as York is an extremely popular destination. Tourist Information Centres will help to find somewhere to stay.

The price codes listed below are based on a standard double room for one night, with breakfast, in peak season. However, prices can fluctuate rapidly, and many hotels will offer special deals like midweek rates, dinner or bed and breakfast packages, so do check their websites first. Out of season prices, especially in winter or during school terms, can also be much cheaper.

£££ over £140
££ £80-£140
£ under £80

Below: the inviting ivy-clad Regency facade of the Grange Hotel.

MINSTER TO OUSEGATE
Dean Court
Duncombe Place; tel: 01904 625082; www.deancourt-york.co.uk.
This comfortable, traditional hotel is very close to the Minster and in its own traffic-free zone. Rooms are decorated in various colour schemes and many have views of the Minster. Its D.C.H. restaurant has 2 AA rosettes. £££

Grays Court
Chapter House Street; tel: 01904 612613; http://grayscourtyork.com.
This stunning historic property started offering accommodation in summer 2010 with five rooms just a stone's throw from the Minster. It's family run and a family home, with a successful mix of contemporary and original features. £££

Judges Lodging
9 Lendal; tel: 01904 638733; www.judgeslodgings.com.
Beautifully refurbished rooms at this elegant and friendly Georgian townhouse, which once provided accommodation for judges visiting the York assizes. Central location makes it a good base for a short break. £££

PAVEMENT
TO TOWER STREET
Hilton Hotel
Tower Street; tel: 01904 648111; www.hilton.co.uk.
If you want a four-star, modern hotel within the City Walls, then the Hilton has contemporary and comfortable rooms, some of which have views of Clifford's Tower. Popular with business travellers too. £££

WEST OF THE OUSE
Cedar Court Grand Hotel
Station Rise; tel: 01904 380038; www.cedarcourtgrand.co.uk.
This five-star hotel opened in spring 2010. Situated in an imposing Edwardian building, once the HQ of the North

Above: the Hodgson's Choice Penthouse 80 offers stunning views of the river and Minster.

Eastern Railway, it brings luxury to the city centre, with a spa, spacious rooms and a personal butler service for those staying in a suite. £££

Royal York
Station Road; tel: 01904 653681; www.principal-hayley.com.
You can't miss this grand Victorian hotel as it's right next to the railway station. It has some imposing public rooms, a mix of contemporary and classic bedrooms, and fine views across the gardens to the cathedral. £££

Hodgson's Choice
80 Postern Close; tel: 01904 610351; www.hodgsons-choice.co.uk.
Close to Skeldergate Bridge is this sleek, 5-star self-catering apartment, which sleeps two adults. Known as Penthouse 80, it has stunning views of the river looking towards York Minster. Minimum stay of three nights. ££

OUTSIDE CITY WALLS
Arnot House
17 Grosvenor Terrace; tel: 01904 641966; www.arnothouseyork.co.uk.
There are just three rooms, and plenty of period features, at this comfortable B&B a short walk from the city centre. Local produce served at breakfast – and vegetarian options too. £

Bishops
135 Holgate Road; tel: 01904 628000; www.bishopsyork.co.uk.
All the rooms are different at this guesthouse in a Victorian villa on the city outskirts – two of the rooms have four-poster beds. There's free Wi-Fi and you take breakfast in the light, sunny dining room. £

Bootham Gardens Guest House
47 Bootham Crescent; tel: 01904 625911; www.bootham-gardens-guesthouse.co.uk.
This purpose-built guesthouse has several ground floor rooms that are suitable for less mobile visitors. There's a guest lounge with a courtyard garden, and free computer access (with Skype). £

Hotel Noir
3 Clifton Green; tel: 0800 612 8008; www.hotelnoir.co.uk.
In various shapes and sizes, the contemporary rooms are all crisp and unfussy in shades of black and white.

Below: staying in a yurt is a fun alternative to camping for the entire family to enjoy.

There is free Wi-Fi too. The hotel is a short walk from the City Walls. £££

The Grange
Clifton; tel: 01904 644744; www.grangehotel.co.uk.
This ivy-clad regency townhouse is just a short walk from the Museum Gardens. It has a restful air, with squashy sofas and open fires in winter. A few rooms have four-poster beds. £££

The Groves
15 St Peters Groves; tel: 01904 559777; www.thegroveshotelyork.co.uk.
Set in a peaceful tree-lined cul-de-sac, a pleasant 10-minute stroll from the city centre, The Groves offers superior bed and breakfast. The main building retains some interesting late Victorian features. Bedrooms come in various shapes and sizes but all have been stylishly refurbished. ££

Mount Royale
The Mount; tel: 01904 628856; www.mountroyale.co.uk.
A good option for families (it has an outdoor heated swimming pool and a pleasant garden), this hotel is comfortable and secluded. It's a short walk to reach Micklegate Bar. ££

Middlethorpe Hall
Near Bishopthorpe; tel: 01904 641241; www.middlethorpe.com.
Friendly staff and excellent service at this elegant country hotel set in a 17th-century house belonging to the National Trust. It's surrounded by glorious gardens and is close to the racecourse. Good bus links take you to the city centre in 15 minutes. £££

WEBSITES
Other useful websites are:
YHA International: www.yha.org.uk
York Yurts: www.yorkyurts.com
York Luxury Holidays: www.yorkluxuryholidays.co.uk
www.bedandbreakfastnationwide.com

Index

Credits

Insight Great Breaks York
Written by: John Scott, Rebecca Ford
Updated by: Jackie Staddon and Hilary Weston
Edited by: Tom Stainer
Picture Manager: Zoë Goodwin
Maps: APA Publications
Publishing Manager: Rachel Fox
Series Editor: Sarah Clark

All images APA William Shaw except; Alamy 18T, 38B, 65, 75, 79B, 83T, 91, 110T,116; Alh1 5BL; Courtesy Barley Hall 30; Bigstock 16B, 19T, 49T, 55B, 72B, 115B, 117T; Courtesy Bootham School 73B; Courtesy Convent bar 61; Courtesy Dig England 80T; Dreamstime 7B, 12/13, 17, 72T, 102T; Fotolia 15, 20B, 52, 92, 115; Gaspa 8T; Gettyimages 45T; Courtesy The Grand Opera House 51; Courtesy The Grange 124; Steven Fruit 88B; Courtesy The Hairy Fig 89; Courtesy Hodgeson's Choice 125; iStockphoto 2/3, 6/7, 10B, 11, 18B, 21, 23, 24T&B, 26, 29, 40T, 43, 62/3, 62T&M&B, 84T&B, 90B, 94, 99, 103, 106, 114T; Courtesy Jollydays camping 126; Jorvik Cenre 5MR, 44, 94T; Mouseman 19B, 108; Macher Mucha 117B; Courtesy Nidderdale Museum 104; Rex Features 107; Courtesy Ripley Castle 102B; Courtesy St Leonards 73T; Tom Smyth 27, 31T, 35T, 64, 110B; Kate Stuart 94B; Courtesy Studley Royal 104B; Kaihsu Tai 79B; Guillaume Tell 83T; Courtesy Theatre Royal 40/41, 74; Topfoto 37, 40M, 66; Courtesy Turkish Baths 118; Visitingeu 36T; Saski van de Nieuwenhof 47; Keep Waddling 32T; York Tourist Board 50, 123.
Cover pictures by: Travel Pictures Ltd (T)
William Shaw/Apa Publications (BL)
Fotolia (BR)

CONTACTING THE EDITORS:
Information has been obtained from sources believed to be reliable, but its accuracy and completeness, and the opinions based thereon, are not guaranteed. We would appreciate it if readers would call our attention to any errors and omissions by contacting: Apa Publications, PO Box 7910, London SE1 1WE, England.
insight@apaguide.co.uk

© 2014 APA Publications (UK) Limited

Second Edition 2014
Printed in China by CTPS

Contains Land-Form Panorama Contours & Meridian 2 and OS Street View data © Crown copyright and database right.

Worldwide distribution enquiries:
APA Publications GmbH & Co. Verlag KG (Singapore Branch)
7030 Ang Mo Kio Ave 5,
08-65 Northstar @ AMK, Singapore 569880
apasin@singnet.com.sg

Distributed in the UK and Ireland by:
Dorling Kindersley Ltd
(a Penguin Company)
80 Strand, London, WC2R 0RL, UK
sales@uk.dk.com